Contemporary's

WORD POWER

Spelling and Vocabulary in Context

Intermediate

1

CB

CONTEMPORARY BOOKS

a division of NTC/CONTEMPORARY PUBLISHING GROUP
Lincolnwood, Illinois USA

Acknowledgments

Page 122: Pronunciation key copyright © 1996 by Houghton Mifflin Company. Reproduced by permission from *The American Heritage Student Dictionary.*

Series Developer
Phil LeFaivre
    Cottage Communications
    Sandwich, Massachusetts

Series Reviewer
Joan Loncich
    Instructor, Adult Basic Education
    Barnstable Community Schools
    Hyannis, Massachusetts

ISBN: 0-8092-0836-9

Published by Contemporary Books,
a division of NTC/Contemporary Publishing Group, Inc.,
4255 West Touhy Avenue,
Lincolnwood (Chicago), Illinois 60712-1975 U.S.A.

15 14   DOH 20 19 18

Market Development Manager

Noreen Lopez

Editorial Development Director

Cynthia Krejcsi

Project Manager

Laurie Duncan

Interior Design and Production

PiperStudiosInc

Cover Design

Kristy Sheldon

Word Power

Table of Contents

To the Teacher

Goals of the Series

Word Power provides the mature learner with a systematic program of instruction for reading, writing, and spelling the words needed on the job, at home, and in the community. The vocabulary is arranged thematically at appropriate levels of difficulty and presented in meaningful contexts.

Key Features

1. Word Power *provides instruction at five levels of difficulty, so you can select the book that precisely fits your students' needs.*

   Each of the five *Word Power* books is keyed to a level of the *Tests of Adult Basic Education*, Forms 7 & 8. The *Introductory Level* correlates with Level L. *Word Power Intermediate 1* and *Intermediate 2* are tied to TABE levels E and M. *Word Power Advanced 1* and *Advanced 2* match levels D and A. The four upper-level books offer a pre-test to confirm appropriateness of level and to provide a comparison for post-test purposes.

2. *Words are presented in meaningful contexts. Students immediately see the importance of what they are studying and become motivated to complete the work successfully.*

   Units in the four upper-level books are keyed to one of six Comprehensive Adult Student Assessment System (CASAS) Life Skills Competencies: Consumer Economics, Health, Employment, Community Resources, Government and Law, and Learning to Learn.

3. *The skills of reading, writing, and spelling are synchronized to facilitate learning and build a portfolio of successful work.*

   Once students have analyzed the meaning and spelling of the words, they can apply what they have learned in a practical writing and proofreading exercise. A number of the letters, announcements, or similar realistic messages that students write can be mailed or kept in a portfolio of each student's work.

4. *Regular review tests in standardized testing formats allow you to monitor progress while familiarizing your students with the testing strategies they will find in typical GED exams and tests of adult basic skills.*

   Every four-lesson unit concludes with a two-page review test. It checks each student's progress in mastering the meaning and spelling of the words. The testing formats match those used by the TABE.

5. *The easy-to-use format and a Mini-Dictionary at the four upper levels empower students to take control of their learning and work with a high degree of independence.*

   Each lesson follows a sequence through four key stages of learning, described on page 8. Students can work independently and progress at their own rate.

6. *The important* Introductory *book provides basic instruction in the key phonetic principles and mechanics skills in a meaningful adult context.*

   Unlike most programs for mature learners, *Word Power* provides instruction in the basic principles of sounds and letters, and it accomplishes this through high-interest, mature content.

Using the Intermediate 1 Book

Like all the books in this series, *Intermediate 1* consists of twenty-four lessons. After each unit of four lessons, a review test is provided to check progress. Each lesson is divided into four one-page parts. Each part brings to closure a coherent step in the learning process. Depending on your students and your instructional time block, one or more parts or an entire lesson might constitute a class session.

The reading level in this book has been carefully controlled, but students may need occasional help with the text. One practical strategy is to work with groups of students, reading the directions aloud to them as they follow along.

The Pre-test on pages 10 and 11 will provide assistance in evaluating how much your students know and placing them in the appropriate *Word Power* text. No single test, however, should serve as the sole guide to placement. Used in conjunction with other tests of reading and writing, as well as your own observations, this Pre-test can serve as a valuable resource. These tests have a multiple-choice format. Random guessing will result in a number of correct answers, so it is wise to expect a high level of mastery before deciding to move students to the next level. In addition, the lessons in this text include many related language skills not covered in the Pre-tests. A better strategy might be to allow students who do well on the Pre-test to progress through the lessons independently at an accelerated pace.

The Post-test on pages 120 and 121 can serve as a handy tool for checking progress. Both tests cover selected words in this text, so a comparison of scores will provide a gauge of each student's progress.

In addition to the Pre-test and Post-test, each text includes a Personal Word List page and a How to Use the Dictionary page. The Personal Word List page allows students to record words encountered outside the classroom. These words can be studied using the steps in How to Study a Word on page 9. They can also be shared and discussed with the class as a means of enhancing each lesson. This is usually best done as part of the writing and proofreading part of the lesson.

The instructions for completing each part are clearly stated and could be performed by many students with a high degree of independence. You may prefer to have students check their own work using the Answer Key on pages 137 through 142. They can record the number correct in the space provided at the bottom of most pages.

As you can see, *Word Power* is an effective and practical tool for addressing the needs of a wide variety of adult learners. We feel confident that *Word Power* will make a significant contribution to your vital work as a teacher.

Breaking Down a Lesson

Each lesson in *Word Power* progresses through the following stages of instruction:

Ⓐ Check the Meaning

Here students read the words in the context of a brief essay related to the unit theme. Students are asked to infer the meanings of the words from the context and match them with one of the definitions provided in the exercise items. These exercises, like most of the exercises in the lessons, lend themselves easily to both independent and cooperative learning.

Ⓑ Study the Spelling

This page contains a wide variety of exercises designed to focus attention on the letters and word parts that make up the spelling of each word. Emphasis is placed on noting coherent clusters of letters, tricky sound/letter combinations, and related and inflected forms of the words.

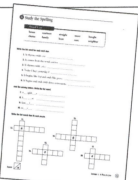

Ⓒ Build Your Skills

Using one or more of the list words as a springboard, this part focuses attention on important language skills, such as recognizing homophones, inflectional endings, prefixes, suffixes, capitalization, and punctuation. Practice activities follow a concise statement of the rule and examples.

Ⓓ Proofread and Write

The lessons conclude by having students apply what they have learned. First students proofread an example of writing related to the lesson theme. Then they correct the errors they find. This is followed by a structured writing assignment modeled on the format they have just proofread. They proofread and correct their own work and make a final copy for their writing portfolios. Cooperative learning strategies can be employed by having students share a draft of their written work with a classmate and solicit his or her response before making the final copy.

How to Study a Word

Follow these steps for learning how to spell new words.

1 **Look** at the word.

- How many syllables does it have?
- Do you know what the word means?

2 **Say** the word aloud.

- What vowel sounds do you hear?
- What consonant sounds do you hear?

3 **Cover** the word.

- Can you see the word in your mind?
- What are the sounds and letters in the word?

4 **Write** the word.

- How is each sound spelled?
- Can you form the letters carefully?

5 **Check** the spelling.

- Did you spell the word correctly?

6 If you make a mistake, repeat the steps.

Pre-test

Part 1: Meaning

For each item below, fill in the letter next to the word or phrase that most nearly expresses the meaning of the first word.

> **Sample**
>
> hammer
>
> (A) part of the arm   (C) a type of vegetable
> ● a tool used for driving nails   (D) to mix thoroughly

1. cautious
- (A) having an unusual look
- (B) careful
- (C) well planned
- (D) full of action

2. peculiar
- (A) tricky
- (B) strange or unusual
- (C) thoughtful
- (D) tasty

3. doubt
- (A) to move quickly
- (B) to be unable to hear
- (C) to change slowly
- (D) to be unsure

4. demand
- (A) a warning
- (B) an important question
- (C) a strong request
- (D) an evil power

5. hostile
- (A) a place to sleep
- (B) unfriendly
- (C) a type of door
- (D) easy or simple

6. achieve
- (A) to blame
- (B) to fool
- (C) to take the place of
- (D) to reach a goal

7. weak
- (A) not strong
- (B) seven days
- (C) thin
- (D) having a sharp edge

8. perfect
- (A) unhappy
- (B) broken
- (C) without mistakes
- (D) sweet

9. survive
- (A) to look over carefully
- (B) to hurry away
- (C) to stay alive
- (D) to wait

10. talent
- (A) something left behind
- (B) a sacred promise
- (C) a type of money
- (D) ability

GO ON ➤

Part 2: Spelling

For each item below, fill in the letter next to the correct spelling of the word.

11. (A) temperture   (C) temprature
    (B) temperature   (D) temperachure

12. (A) belief   (C) beleif
    (B) balief   (D) beleef

13. (A) propur   (C) propar
    (B) propper   (D) proper

14. (A) libary   (C) libarey
    (B) library   (D) libbary

15. (A) necessary   (C) necessarey
    (B) nessasary   (D) necesary

16. (A) perforum   (C) perform
    (B) purform   (D) preform

17. (A) familar   (C) familier
    (B) familiar   (D) familiur

18. (A) devosion   (C) devotion
    (B) devoshun   (D) davotion

19. (A) ramember   (C) remembur
    (B) remember   (D) rimembre

20. (A) squeeze   (C) squeaze
    (B) squeze   (D) squeez

21. (A) revue   (C) review
    (B) raview   (D) reveiw

22. (A) sircl   (C) cirkle
    (B) circle   (D) cercle

23. (A) height   (C) hieght
    (B) hite   (D) hight

24. (A) peace   (C) pease
    (B) peece   (D) paece

25. (A) anser   (C) antser
    (B) answur   (D) answer

26. (A) rinkle   (C) wrinkle
    (B) wrenkle   (D) wrinkel

27. (A) jale   (C) jaile
    (B) jayle   (D) jail

28. (A) enuf   (C) enouf
    (B) enough   (D) enugh

29. (A) baddle   (C) battle
    (B) batle   (D) battel

30. (A) lease   (C) laese
    (B) liese   (D) leese

STOP

A Place to Live

A Check the Meaning

Read the paragraph below. Think about the meaning of the words in bold type.

Should you buy or **rent** a place to live? The **choice** affects everyone in your **family**. It is, therefore, wise to be very **cautious** when making this decision. If you buy a **house**, you need a lot of money to begin with. This money is called the down payment. After you have **bought** the house, it will not be easy to **move** to another place. If you do not like a **neighbor**, there is little you can do. Someone who rents, on the other hand, can move when the **lease** is up. A renter does not have to make a large down payment. Yet renting has its drawbacks. Money spent on rent goes **straight** to the owner. It is gone forever. Money spent buying a house gives people something for their money.

Write each word in bold type next to its meaning. Check your answers in the Mini-Dictionary.

Cautious **1.** taking great care to avoid a mistake

Lease **2.** an agreement between a property owner and a renter

Move **3.** to change the place where you live

bought **4.** the past form of *buy*; gave money for something

Straight **5.** without a break or a bend; direct

Rent **6.** to pay money to live in someone's property

Neighbor **7.** someone who lives nearby

house **8.** a building people live in

Family **9.** people who live together in a house

Choice **10.** the act of choosing between two or more things

B Study the Spelling

Word List

house	cautious	straight	move	bought
choice	family	lease	rent	neighbor

Write the list word for each clue.

1. It rhymes with *sent.* _rent_

2. It comes from the word *caution.* _Cautious_

3. It rhymes with *voice.* _Choice_

4. Today I buy; yesterday I _bought_ .

5. It begins like *leaf* and ends like *grease.* _Lease._

6. It begins and ends with three consonants. _Straight_

Add the missing letters. Write the list word.

7. n_e_ighb_o_r _neighbor_

8. h_o__u_se _house_

9. fam_i_l_y_ _family._

10. m_o_v_e_ _move._

Write the list words that fit each puzzle.

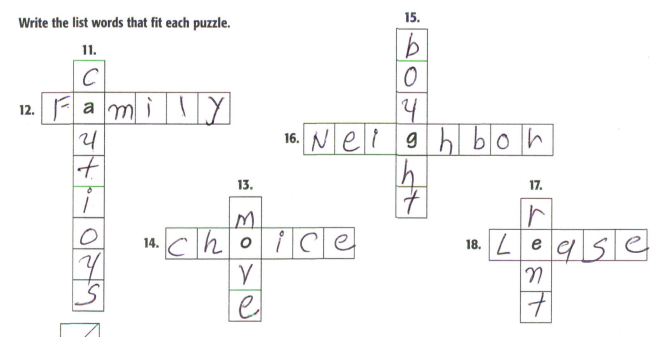

Score: __ / 18

Ⓒ Build Your Skills

Language Tutor

A dictionary lists words in alphabetical, or ABC, order. Words beginning with *a* come before words beginning with *b*. If the first letter is the same, compare the second letter of each word.

A B C D E F G H I J K L M N O P Q R S T U V W X Y Z

The words in each column below are in alphabetical order.

animal	lease	cautious
bought	move	choice
cautious	neighbor	family

Write each group of words in alphabetical order.

1. rent   move   family

Family
Move
rent.

2. apple   grape   lemon

apple.
grape.
lemon.

3. stand   sit   bend

bend
sit
stand.

4. money   lease   map

Lease
map
money

5. house   hill   yard

hill
house
yard.

6. straight   break   bake

bake
break
straight

7. car   check   clerk

car
check
clerk

8. room   rail   rub

rail
room
rub.

Score: 8

D Proofread and Write

Ramon wants to rent a place to live, Here is a list of questions Ramon made to ask the owner, He made three spelling mistakes, Cross out the misspelled words. Write the correct spellings above them.

> **Questions to ask the owner:**
>
> How much is the rent?
>
> Who lives in the ~~house~~ next door?
> *house*
>
> Is my ~~nieghbor~~ quiet?
> *Neighbor*
>
> Can I get a two-year ~~leese?~~
> *Leese. ?*
>
> Do I get a choice of colors when you paint?
>
> How soon can my family and I move in?

Make a list of questions you would ask before renting or buying a place to live.
Use at least three list words.

_____

_____

_____

_____

_____

_____

_____

Writing Portfolio

Proofread your list carefully. Correct any mistakes. Then make a clean copy and put it in your writing portfolio.

Dollars and Good Sense

(A) Check the Meaning

Read the paragraph below. Think about the meaning of the words in bold type.

Getting the best buy will **require** that you compare prices. Take **dairy** products, for example. A four-**ounce** stick of ABC **butter** costs fifty cents. A one-pound box of XYZ butter costs $2.50. Do not **guess** which price is lower. Check the price for the same unit. How much is a stick of XYZ butter? Suppose that a **quart** of milk costs seventy-five cents. Is it smart to buy two pints at fifty cents each? The amount of milk you **receive** will be the same. Which costs less: $2.25 for a five-pound bag of **sugar**, or a two-pound box of sugar cubes for $1.85? Some people are careful never to waste a **crumb** of cake. Yet they pay too much for the **flour** they use to bake it.

Write each word in bold type next to its meaning. Check your answers in the Mini-Dictionary.

Sugar   **1.** a sweet-tasting item used as food

Quart.   **2.** a unit for measuring liquid; equal to two pints

require.   **3.** to demand or need

dairy.   **4.** having to do with milk and milk products

Crumb.   **5.** a tiny piece of food

receive.   **6.** to get or gain

~~stop~~ guess.   **7.** to decide something without much study,

Flour.   **8.** a powder made from grain and used in baking

ounce.   **9.** a unit of weight; one sixteenth of a pound

butter.   **10.** a soft, fatty food made from cream

B Study the Spelling

Word List

require	quart	guess	dairy	butter
crumb	flour	ounce	receive	sugar

Write the list word or words for each clue.

1. They have a double consonant in their spelling.
   butter   *guess*

2. It rhymes with *hairy*. *dairy*

3. They begin with two consonants.
   crumb   *Flour*

4. There is an *ei* in its spelling. *receive*

5. It sounds like *flower* but has a different meaning. *Flour*

6. It begins like *out* and ends like *once*. *ounce*

7. They begin with *re*. *require*   *receive*

Replace the underlined letters. Write a list word.

8. <u>de</u>ceive *receive*   11. <u>f</u>airy *Dairy*

9. <u>s</u>uper *sugar*   12. qua<u>ke</u> *quart*

10. gue<u>st</u> *guess*   13. <u>bu</u>zzer *butter*

One word in each group is misspelled. Circle the misspelled word. Write it correctly.

14. (quess)   quart   dairy   *guess*

15. (raquire)   receive   crumb   *require*

Add the missing letter. Write a list word.

16. crum_b_ *crumb*

17. g_u_ess *guess*

18. d_a_ _i_ry *dairy*

Score: / 18

C Build Your Skills

Language Tutor

Words are made up of parts called *syllables*. A syllable has one vowel sound.
Say these words. Listen for the syllables.

One syllable:	crumb	
Two syllables:	butter	but•ter
Three syllables:	tomorrow	to•mor•row

Look up these words in your Mini-Dictionary. Write each word. Use dots between the syllables.
Circle any word with one syllable.

1. choice _cho.ice choice – ①_
2. sugar _su.gar – ②_
3. (dairy) _dairy dai.ry – ②_
4. require _re.qu.ire re-quire – ②_
5. (house) _house – ①_
6. family _fa.mi.ly – ③_
7. (rent) _rent – ①_
8. receive _re.ce.ive re-ceive ②_

Write these words. Use dots between the syllables.

9. body _body bo-dy_
10. guess _guess – ①_
11. enough _en.ough_
12. before _be.fore ②_
13. fish _Fish ①_
14. bacon _ba.con ②_
15. window _win-dow ②_

16. yellow _Yellow ②_
17. sandwich _Sand.wich ②_
18. dark _dark ①_
19. member _mem-ber ②_
20. husband _hus-band ①_
21. happiness _happi-ness ③_
22. afternoon _after-noon ③_

Score: ___/22

Ⓓ Proofread and Write

Meg wrote this letter to a store manager. She asked the manager to put unit prices on all items. Meg made three spelling mistakes. Cross out the misspelled words. Write the correct spellings above them.

399 Stone St.

Acton, ME 04001

December 3, 1997

Ms. Amy Dix

Farm Market

555 First St.

Acton, ME 04001

Dear Ms. Dix:

It would help shoppers if you put unit prices on everything. Now I must guess which brand costs less. Please list the price per ounce for all diary items like butter. Show milk prices by the qart. Flour and sugar can be priced by the pound. The law does not require this. However, it would help the buyer recieve the best value.

{ dairy.
quart.
receive. }

Sincerely,

Meg Jones

Meg Jones

Writing Portfolio

Write a letter to a store manager. Use your own paper. Suggest a way to improve the store. Use at least three list words.

Proofread your letter carefully and correct any mistakes. Then make a clean copy and mail it to the business or put it in your writing portfolio.

A Good Fit

Ⓐ Check the Meaning

Read the paragraph below. Think about the meaning of the words in bold type.

Buying the right clothes can be tricky. Most of us think first about **style**. Pants must have the right cuff. A shirt must have the latest **collar**. Anyone who wears an **unfamiliar** style is thought to be **peculiar**. Yet there are other things to think about, such as fit. A good fit is not just a matter of **weight** and **height**. One's body type is more important. Someone who lifts heavy loads will have a larger chest and arms. Tight-fitting clothes like **jeans** should allow **enough** room to move or grow. Remember, most clothes will **shrink** after you wash and dry them. Also think about how much care the clothes will need. Some will **wrinkle** easily and need to be ironed often. The right clothes will look good and be easy to care for.

Write each word in bold type next to its meaning. Check your answers in the Mini-Dictionary.

enough.   **1.** as much as needed (ઇનફ)

style.   **2.** a special way of doing something, especially with clothes

unfamiliar.   **3.** not seen or heard often; unknown

Jeans   **4.** pants made from denim or another strong, heavy cloth

wrinkle.   **5.** to fold or crease cloth

collar   **6.** a band of cloth around the neckline of a shirt, blouse, or dress

~~weight~~ _height_   **7.** the distance from top to bottom

peculiar   **8.** unusual or strange

~~shirt~~ _shrink_   **9.** to become smaller as the result of water or heat

weight.   **10.** heaviness

Score: /10

B Study the Spelling

Word List

weight	jeans	enough	collar	peculiar
wrinkle	unfamiliar	style	shrink	height

Add the missing syllable. Write the list word.

1. col_lar_ *collar*
2. pecu_liar_ *Peculiar*
3. e_nough_ *enough*
4. unfa_miliar_iar *unfamiliar*

Write the list word or words for each clue.

5. It ends with *s* and has one syllable. *Jeans*
6. They have an *ei* in their spelling. *weight*
7. They end with *le*.
   wrinkle   *style*
8. Five of its six letters are consonants. *shrink*
9. They end with *liar*.
   Peculiar   *unfamiliar*
10. There is a double consonant in its spelling. _____
11. It rhymes with *twinkle*. *wrinkle*
12. These two words come first in alphabetical order.
   collar   *enough*
13. It begins like *shrimp* and ends like *pink*. *wrinkle*

Write the list words with just one syllable.

14. *Jeans*   17. *height*
15. *collar*   18. _____
16. *height*

Score: ⬜/18

C Build Your Skills

Language Tutor

Some words sound alike, but they have different spellings and meanings. The underlined words sound the same. They do not have the same meaning or spelling.

Try a diet to lose <u>weight</u>. I had to <u>wait</u> an hour for the bus.
The heat will melt the <u>lead</u>. A band <u>led</u> the parade.
Ellen is a <u>dear</u> friend. A herd of <u>deer</u> ran among the trees.
The boards <u>creak</u> under my feet. A little <u>creek</u> runs down the hill.
The cut will <u>heal</u> in a week. The <u>heel</u> of my shoe came off.
I will be <u>here</u> at noon. Did you <u>hear</u> what I said?

Write these sentences. Add the correct word in parentheses.

1. The (lead; led) used in some paint is harmful.

The _____ used in some paint is harmful.

2. Burns take a long time to (heal; heel).

Burns take a long time to _____.

3. Willie is such a (dear; deer) child.

Willie is such a _____ child.

4. I cannot (weight; wait) another minute.

I cannot wait another minute.

5. Dr. Martin Luther King, Jr. (lead; led) the fight for civil rights.

Dr. Martin Luther King, Jr _____ the fight for civil rights.

6. We will start the meeting when everyone is (here; hear).

We will start the meeting when everyone is here.

7. We heard the (creak; creek) of the old wooden boat.

We heard the _____ of the old wooden boat.

8. I caught my (heal; heel) and fell down the step.

I caught my _____ and fell down the step.

Score: ___ / 8

⑪ Proofread and Write

Eve is helping her sister with the washing. Her sister left this note for her. She made three spelling mistakes. Cross out the misspelled words. Write the correct spellings above them.

Eve:

collar

The ~~coller~~ on my blouse is very dirty. Use a little

bleach on it. A half cup should be enough. Do not

put my jeans in the dryer. They will shrink. I have

put on some weight, so this could be a problem.

If you see a ~~wrinkel~~ in Fred's shirt, just hang up

wrinkle

the shirt. Have you ever seen such ~~peculyar~~ *peculiar.*

socks? He says they are the style now.

Thanks for your help.

Sis

Writing Portfolio

Write a note to someone on another piece of paper. Tell the person how you like your clothes washed. Use at least three list words.

Proofread your note carefully and correct any mistakes. Then make a clean copy and put it in your writing portfolio.

Following Instructions

(A) Check the Meaning

Read the paragraph below. Think about the meaning of the words in bold type.

Always follow these washing instructions:

1. Before putting clothes into a **machine**, be sure the machine is level.

2. Place your **laundry** in the machine. Be sure to take all keys or change from pockets in shirts and **trousers**. A **coin** can harm the tub of the machine.

3. Add a small amount of soap. Turn the water dial to hot, warm, or cold. The dial may **already** be on the one you want. Then there is no need to change it.

4. Put quarters, dimes, or nickels in the slot. It will not take a **penny**. The clerk can make change for a **dollar**.

5. If the washer begins to **vibrate** or **bounce**, turn it off. Check to see if it is level.

6. Look through the **window** in the door. You will see your clothes getting clean.

Write each word in bold type next to its meaning. Check your answers in the Mini-Dictionary.

dollar   **1.** paper money equal to one hundred cents

already   **2.** by this time; earlier

Laundry   **3.** clothes to be washed

penny   **4.** a one-cent piece

bounce   **5.** to move about; to spring up and down

vibrate   **6.** to move back and forth very rapidly

Machine   **7.** a tool or piece of equipment that does a job

coin   **8.** a piece of metal used as money

trousers   **9.** pants or slacks

window   **10.** an opening usually covered with glass

B Study the Spelling

Word List

vibrate	already	bounce	trousers	machine
dollar	coin	penny	laundry	window

Add the missing letters. Write the list word.

1. dol_l_a_r *dollar*
2. pen_ny *penny*
3. la_u_nd_r_y *laundry*
4. bo_u_n_c_e *bounce*
5. ma_c_h_i_ne *machine*
6. c_o_i_n *coin.*

Write the list word or words for each clue.

7. It has three syllables and ends with *y*. *already*
8. It rhymes with *collar*. *dollar*
9. It has the word *ready* in its spelling. *already*
10. They have a double consonant in their spelling.
    dollar , *penny*
11. It has the word *wind* in its spelling. *window.*
12. It begins like *vine* and ends like *celebrate*. *vibrate.*
13. It begins with two consonants. *Trousers*
14. They have just one syllable. *dollar* *penny*
    bounce *coin*

Write the list words with two syllables. Use dots between the syllables.

15. *vibrate.*
16. *machine.*
17. *window*
18. *laundry.*
19. *penny*
20. *dollar.*

C Build Your Skills

Language Tutor

Add *-s* to most words to make them mean "more than one." The new word is called a *plural*.

Singular	Plural	Singular	Plural
window	windows	coin	coins
dollar	dollars	machine	machines

Add *-es* to words ending with *-s, -ch, -sh,* or *-x* to make them plural.

Singular	Plural	Singular	Plural
dress	dresses	church	churches
dish	dishes	fox	foxes

Write each sentence. Change the underlined word from singular to plural.

1. The <u>machine</u> take only dimes.

The machines take only dimes.

2. Come early and bring your <u>toolbox</u>.

Come early and bring your toolboxes.

3. Follow the <u>direction</u> carefully.

Follow the directions carefully.

4. Help me wash these <u>dish</u>.

Help me wash these dishes.

5. The high winds blew several <u>branch</u> off the tree.

The high winds blew several branches off the tree.

6. Fold the <u>shirt</u> and put them in the basket.

Fold the shirts and put them in the basket

7. I spent too much for those <u>glass</u>.

I spent too much for those glasses

8. The <u>house</u> vibrate when a train passes.

The houses vibrate when a train passes.

D Proofread and Write

The Wash & Dry Shop has these signs on the walls. There are three spelling mistakes on the signs.
Cross out the misspelled words. Write the correct spellings above them.

Do not put too

much ~~landry~~ in a
Laundry
machine.

Some trousers were
found last night.

See the owner.

Keep metal carts **away**
from the window.
already
One has ~~allready~~ been
broken this week.

Make sure your load is level.
If not, machines will bounce and vibrate.

dollar.
There is a one-~~doller~~ charge

for leaving clothes overnight.

(Pockets)

Make up your own rules or directions for washing clothes. Use at least three list words.

Before putting clothes check ~~clothes~~ *(pockets)*
before start machine checks level.
machine started after virbate then ~~stop~~ stop.
machine's window close After start machine.
~~Cloth clean After~~ *then* move the Drymachine.

Writing Portfolio

**Proofread your rules carefully. Correct any mistakes. Then make a clean copy and put
it in your writing portfolio.**

Unit 1 Review

Finish the Meaning

Fill in the circle next to the word that best completes each sentence.

Sample

The plane will be late. The _____ was caused by bad weather.

● delay   Ⓒ worry
Ⓑ rain   Ⓓ anger

1. We need to buy more milk. You will find it in the _____ case.

   Ⓐ laundry   ● dairy
   Ⓑ sugar   Ⓓ trousers

2. He painted his house blue and orange. It looks quite _____.

   Ⓐ cautious   Ⓒ enough
   ● peculiar   Ⓓ straight

3. Grapes cost twenty-five cents a pound. The clerk must check their _____.

   ● weight   Ⓒ machine
   Ⓑ choice   Ⓓ style

4. Everyone must wear a hard hat. The work rules _____ it.

   Ⓐ guess   Ⓒ move
   ● require   Ⓓ vibrate

5. I have four brothers and six sisters. We have a large _____.

   Ⓐ collar   Ⓒ choice
   Ⓑ style   ● family

6. These pants are too large. I hope they _____ when they are washed.

   ● shrink   Ⓒ bounce
   Ⓑ move   Ⓓ rent

7. The children ate all the cake. Not a _____ was left.

   Ⓐ coin   Ⓒ crumb
   Ⓑ sugar   ● quart

8. The shirt pinched my neck. The _____ was too small.

   Ⓐ weight   ● collar
   Ⓑ laundry   Ⓓ choice

9. The planes fly low over the house. My walls _____ all day.

   ● vibrate   Ⓒ guess
   Ⓑ shrink   Ⓓ require

10. This _____ needs both oil and gas to work.

   Ⓐ window   ● machine
   Ⓑ house   Ⓓ quart

GO ON ➡

Check the Spelling

Fill in the circle next to the word that is spelled correctly and best completes each sentence.

11. The _____ of that fence is three feet.

Ⓐ hite   ● height

Ⓑ heit   Ⓓ hieght

12. Always read a _____ carefully before signing it.

Ⓐ leese   Ⓒ liese

● lease   Ⓓ leace

13. A well-made bed will not show a single _____.

● wrinkle   Ⓒ wrinkel

Ⓑ rinkle   Ⓓ wrenkle

14. We will need more _____ to make this cake.

Ⓐ flowr   Ⓒ flouer

Ⓑ fluor   ● flour

15. Please give me change for a _____.

Ⓐ doller   Ⓒ daller

Ⓑ doler   ● dollar

16. Harry went _____ to the beach after work.

Ⓐ streight   Ⓒ straight

Ⓑ strate   Ⓓ straite

17. How much does a twelve-_____ bottle of soda cost?

● ounce   Ⓒ ounse

Ⓑ ownce   Ⓓ ownse

18. We often _____ our mail in the morning.

Ⓐ recieve   Ⓒ receeve

● receive   Ⓓ resieve

19. When we got there, the game had _____ started.

Ⓐ allready   Ⓒ allredy

Ⓑ alredy   ● already

20. Our _____ helped us shovel after the snowstorm.

Ⓐ naybor   Ⓒ naghbor

● neighbor   Ⓓ nieghbor

STOP

Score: _____ / 20

Getting a Checkup

A Check the Meaning

Read the paragraph below. Think about the meaning of the words in bold type.

Some jobs require that workers pass a health exam of some kind. Sometimes this checkup can tell **whether** the worker is able to do a job. Workers who lift heavy loads must be strong. A worker with a **weak knee** or a bad **back** might hurt himself or **another** worker. People who work with food may face a different kind of exam. They may be checked to be sure they have not **caught** an illness that could spread to others. A nurse may take a worker's body **temperature**. Or a doctor may look at the **tongue** for signs of ill health. Someone who drives a car or truck must have his or her **eyes** tested from time to time. Most of these checkups are **brief**, taking only ten to fifteen minutes. Yet they are important for workers' good health.

Write each word in bold type next to its meaning. Check your answers in the Mini-Dictionary.

Caught. 1. the past form of _catch_, meaning "to grab or become ill with"

weak knee 2. not having power, energy, or strength

brief 3. short; not long

knee 4. the part of the body where the upper and lower leg come together

whether. 5. if

tongue. 6. the fleshy organ in the mouth used for eating and speaking

eyes 7. the part of the body used for seeing

another. 8. different or additional

back 9. the part of the body opposite the chest that reaches from the neck to the hips

temperature. 10. hotness or coldness, especially of the body

Score: / 10

B Study the Spelling

Word List

brief	whether	weak	knee	another
temperature	tongue	eyes	back	caught

Write a list word or words for each clue.

1. It begins with a silent *k*. _knee_
2. It has the word *other* in it. _another_
3. There is an *ie* in its spelling. _brief_
4. It rhymes with *taught*. _tongue caught_
5. It is plural. _eyes_
6. They end with *er*. _whether_ _another_
7. It has four syllables. _temperature_
8. It rhymes with *track*. _back_
9. It ends with a silent *ue*. _tongue_
10. Change one letter in *leak* to make this word. _weak_

Write the list words with just one syllable. Circle the one-syllable words that begin with two consonants.

11. _brief_
12. _Caught_
13. _back_
14. _eyes_
15. _weak_
16. _knee_
17. _tongue_

Add the missing letters. Write the list words.

18. e_yes_ _eyes_
19. cau_ght_ _Caught_
20. tong_ue_ _tongue_
21. temper_atu_re _temperature_
22. w_h_eth_e_r _whether_

Score: ___/22

C Build Your Skills

Language Tutor

Some words have silent letters. You may not hear these letters when you say the word, but they are needed in spelling.

caught   knee   tongue

Read these sentences. Write the underlined word and circle the silent letter.

1. Do not <u>climb</u> on the rocks. _climb (clim)_

2. I <u>listen</u> to music on my way to work. _Listen (Lis en)_

3. Be sure to <u>answer</u> all the questions. _answer (ans er)_

4. We took the <u>wrong</u> road. _wrong (rong)_

5. The cow looked after her <u>calf</u>. _Calf (caf)_

6. I hurt my <u>thumb</u> at work. _thumb (thum)_

7. Always pay your <u>debts</u> on time. _debts (dets)_

8. I need a pair of <u>scissors</u> to cut the tape. _scissors (sissors)_

9. I wear a watch on my <u>wrist</u>. _wrist (rist)_

10. The <u>knob</u> on the door was broken. _knob (nob)_

11. Please tie the rope in a <u>knot</u>. _knot (not)_

12. We visited the old <u>castle</u>. _Castle (casle)_

13. It was an <u>honor</u> to carry the flag. _honor (onor)_

14. He likes to <u>knit</u> and sew. _knit (nit)_

15. The bird sat on the <u>limb</u> of the tree. _Limb (clim)_

16. Mary had a little <u>lamb</u>. _Lamb (lam)_

17. Have you ever seen a <u>ghost</u>? _ghost? (gost)_

18. Eve scraped a <u>knuckle</u>. _knuckle (nuckle)_

19. Read the <u>sign</u> on the wall. _sign (sin)_

20. Be my <u>guest</u> for lunch. _guest (gest)_

      Score: /20

ⓓ Proofread and Write

Ken had an accident at work and had to write a report. He made three spelling mistakes. Cross out the misspelled words. Write the correct spellings above them.

A C C I D E N T   R E P O R T

Bud's Food Service

Report Filed by: Ken Simpson

Date of Accident: April 17, 1998   **Place of Accident:** Kitchen

Nature of Accident: Something did not work right on the oven. In a very brief time, the temperture reached 475 degrees. A rag left near the oven cought fire. The smoke got in my eyes and made me week. It also caused a bad taste in my mouth and on my tongue. I had to lie down for a time. I will see a doctor in the morning. He will tell me whether I should come back to work tomorrow.

Caught, temperature, weak,

Write a report about an accident that happened at home or on the job. It can be a real accident or one you make up. Use at least three list words.

Writing Portfolio

Proofread your report carefully. Correct any mistakes. Then make a clean copy and put it in your writing portfolio.

6 Staying Healthy

Ⓐ Check the Meaning

Read the paragraph below. Think about the meaning of the words in bold type.

As someone once said, "If I had known I was going to live so long, I would have taken better **care** of myself." If you take care of your **body** now, it will take care of you later. Make it a **habit** to ride a **bicycle** or run every day. Some exercises can be done quite easily. While you ride the bus, **squeeze** a ball with your **fingers** and stretch your neck and chin. You do not need to tire yourself. Just **repeat** the exercise several times. A muscle that is **seldom** used will soon become weak. A cut that is neglected may cause trouble, too, by becoming infected. Treat it right away. **Bathe** the cut thoroughly to clean out any germs. Then see a doctor or visit a **clinic**.

Write each word in bold type next to its meaning. Check your answers in the Mini-Dictionary.

_____ **1.** the five parts of the body attached to the palm of the hand

_____ **2.** a place that offers medical help

_____ **3.** an action done so often it is done without thinking about it

_____ **4.** to wash in order to clean

_____ **5.** to look after; to protect

_____ **6.** the whole or physical part of a person

_____ **7.** not often

_____ **8.** something used to move about that is driven by pushing pedals

_____ **9.** to say or do more than once

_____ **10.** to press together very hard

B Study the Spelling

Word List				
squeeze	seldom	bicycle	body	habit
finger	care	clinic	repeat	bathe

Form a list word by matching the beginning of a word in the first column with its ending in the second column. Write the list word.

sel	peat	1. _____
bod	ic	2. _____
clin	cycle	3. _____
hab	y	4. _____
fin	dom	5. _____
bi	it	6. _____
re	ger	7. _____

Write a list word for each clue.

8. It has seven letters but just one syllable. _____

9. It has just four letters and two syllables. _____

10. Add one letter to *bath* to form this word. _____

11. It rhymes with *stare*. _____

12. It begins like *repay* and ends like *defeat*. _____

13. It begins with two consonants and ends with one consonant.

_____

14. It has three syllables. _____

15. Change one letter in *linger* to form this word. _____

Five list words begin with *b* or *c*. Write these words in alphabetical order.

16. _____   19. _____

17. _____   20. _____

18. _____

Score: ___/20

C Build Your Skills

Language Tutor

New words can be formed by adding *-ed* or *-ing* to many verbs.

repeat + -ed = repeated   repeat + -ing = repeating

lift + -ed = lifted   lift + -ing = lifting

walk + -ed = walked   walk + -ing = walking

Add the ending to each word. Write a new word.

1. look + -ed =
_____

2. ask + -ing =
_____

3. add + -ing =
_____

4. stay + -ed =
_____

5 talk + -ed =
_____

6. wash + -ing =
_____

7. mix + -ed =
_____

8. pour + -ing =
_____

9. guess + -ed =
_____

10. boil + -ing =
_____

11. shrink + -ing =
_____

12. explain + -ed =
_____

Write each sentence. Add *-ed* or *-ing* to the underlined word.

13. We <u>ask</u> the crew leader for the day off yesterday.

_____

14. She <u>rush</u> to the clinic to get help an hour ago.

_____

15. Try <u>do</u> some exercises every day.

_____

16. The nurse <u>repeat</u> the directions several times.

_____

D Proofread and Write

Juanita kept a written record of some things she does to stay healthy. She made three spelling mistakes. Cross out the misspelled words. Write the correct spellings above them.

Tuesday

Rode my bicycel for thirty minutes.

Went to the clinic to have my eyes checked.

Wednesday

Lifted weights to make my upper body strong.

Thursday

Had to bath my sprained wrist.

Tried to repeat Tuesday's exercises. My

wrist hurt too much. I could not squeze the

handlebars.

Friday

Decided to stop the habit of eating

between meals.

Writing Portfolio

Make a list of things you try to do to stay healthy. Use your own paper. Include at least three list words.

Proofread your list carefully. Correct any mistakes. Then make a clean copy and put it in your writing portfolio.

Fire Safety

(A) Check the Meaning

Read the paragraph below. Think about the meaning of the words in bold type.

Every year hundreds of children suffer a bad **burn** at home. The careless use of matches or the kitchen stove can cause a **tragedy**. A burn can destroy several layers of **skin**. It can take months or years for a child to **recover**. A burn also holds the **peril** of infection and even death. However, a few simple steps can reduce the **risk** of burns. First, **clean** the oven and stove thoroughly. Grease can easily burst into flames. Never let a child **assist** you by carrying pans of hot liquids. Remember to always keep matches out of reach. Also, place a hot iron upright with plenty of **support** when it is not in use. Finally, keep the number of the fire department near the phone. Firefighters are trained to **rescue** people from fires. They also can give first aid for burns.

Write each word in bold type next to its meaning. Check your answers in the Mini-Dictionary.

recover **1.** to get back something, such as one's health

peril **2.** danger; chance for harm

risk (rescue) **3.** to save from some danger

burn **4.** an injury caused by fire or heat

skin **5.** the covering of a person's or an animal's body

clean **6.** to make free of dirt and grime

assist **7.** to help or aid

support **8.** a thing that holds something up or keeps it from falling

Tragedy **9.** something terrible

risk **10.** the chance of something harmful happening

Score: / 10

Ⓑ Study the Spelling

Word List

support	rescue	burn	recover	tragedy
risk	assist	peril	clean	skin

Write the list word or words for each clue.

1. They have a double consonant in their spelling.

   rescue   *recover*

2. The word *cover* is in its spelling. *recover*

3. It rhymes with *mean*. *clean*

4. The word *tragic* comes from this word. *tragedy*

5. The word *assistant* is made from this word. *assist*

6. It rhymes with *turn*. *burn*

Replace the underlined letters. Write a list word.

7. thin *skin*

8. barn *burn*

9. clear *clean*

10. disk *risk*

Add the missing letters. Write a list word.

11. p_e_r_i_l *peril*

12. r_e_s_C_ue *rescue.*

Write the list word that fits each shape.

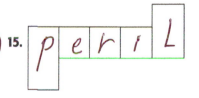

13. *Support*

14. *support*

15. *peril*

16. *recover*

C Build Your Skills

Language Tutor

When a word ends with *e*, the *e* is usually dropped before adding *-ed* or *-ing*.

rescue + -ed = rescued   rescue + -ing = rescuing

When a one-syllable word ends with a vowel and a consonant, the consonant is usually doubled before adding *-ed* or *-ing*.

ship + -ed = shipped   ship + -ing = shipping

Add the endings to these words.

1. dance + -ing = _dance_

2. grab + -ing = _grabing_

3. rub + -ed = _rubbd_

4. please + -ed = _Pleused_

5. care + -ing = _careing_

6. wrap + -ed = _wrapped._

Write these sentences. Add the ending to the underlined word.

7. The cook was squeeze + -ing the juice from the lemons.

_____

8. She spot + -ed the water boiling on the stove.

_____

9. The hot grease drop + -ed on the stove.

The hot grease droppd on the stove

10. Smoke began rise + -ing from the trash.

Smok began rising from the trash.

11. People began run + -ing for the doors.

_____

12. The flames were whip + -ed by the winds.

whipped

Ⓓ Proofread and Write

The kitchen of the café where Peggy worked had this fire-safety poster on the wall. The poster has three spelling mistakes. It also has a mistake in adding *-ing* to a word. Cross out the mistakes. Write the correct spellings above them.

We need your su~~p~~ort.

support

Only you can stop the tragady of a fire!

- Clean the oven and stove every time you use it.
- Keep anything that will burn away from the gas flames.
- ~~Asist~~ a fellow worker in moving hot items.
- Do not risk geting your clothes on fire.
- Keep apron strings tied ~~tightly~~.
- The phone number of the nearest rescue team is 911.

Writing Portfolio

Make a safety list for a babysitter on another piece of paper. Use at least three list words.

Proofread your list carefully. Correct any mistakes. Then make a clean copy and put it in your writing portfolio.

Eat Right

Ⓐ Check the Meaning

Read the paragraph below. Think about the meaning of the words in bold type.

Nowadays, more people are eating fast food. **Instead** of eating **fruit**, such as an orange or a **banana**, they grab the **familiar** hamburger, fries, and maybe something **sweet** like ice cream. These foods fill the **stomach**, but they **contain** a lot of fat and few of the things the human body needs. There are six food groups. The largest one is the bread group. It includes foods made from **grain**: rice, **cereal**, and noodles. One should eat six to eleven servings from this **category** every day. The other categories are fruits and vegetables, meat, dairy foods, and fats. People should limit the amount of meat, fat, and oil they eat every day. Eating right is not always easy, but it is smart.

Write each word in bold type next to its meaning. Check your answers in the Mini-Dictionary.

Cereal. Grain **1.** the seed of wheat, corn, rice, and other food plants

stomach **2.** the part of the body where food goes after it has been eaten

instead. **3.** in place of something

Fruit **4.** the part of a plant that can be eaten, such as an apple or a peach

Category **5.** a group or part of a larger group

banana **6.** a soft fruit with a yellow peel

Familiar. **7.** seen or heard often; well-known

Sweet. **8.** having a pleasant, sugary taste

cereal. **9.** a food made from the seeds of wheat, oats, rice, or corn

Contain **10.** to hold; to be made up of

B Study the Spelling

Word List

sweet	grain	banana	category	cereal
instead	fruit	familiar	contain	stomach

Write the words with one syllable. Circle the vowels in each word.

1. _sweet_
2. _Fruit_

3. _____

Write the words with two syllables. Use dots between the syllables.

4. _____

6. _____

5. _____

Write the list word for each clue.

7. It has three syllables. The last syllable is *iar*. _Familiar_

8. The word *real* is part of its spelling. _Cereal_

9. The first syllable is *cat*. _Category_

10. It has three syllables. The second syllable is *nan*. _banana._

11. It rhymes with *feet*. _Sweet_

12. It begins like *connect* and ends like *stain*. _Contain_

13. It begins like *fresh* and ends like *recruit*. _____

14. The word *rain* is part of its spelling. _grain_

One word in each group is misspelled. Circle the misspelled word. Write it correctly.

15. banana   ⟨stomack⟩   sweet   _Stomach._
16. ⟨insted⟩   grain   cereal   _Instead._
17. cereal   fruit   ⟨familier⟩   _Familiar._
18. ⟨catagory⟩   sweet   contain   _Category._

Score: ☐/18

C Build Your Skills

Language Tutor

If a word ends with a consonant and a *y*, change the *y* to *i* when adding *-es* or *-ed*.

category + -es = categories   study + -ed = studied

Add the endings to the words.

1. city + -es = ~~cittes~~ *cities.*

2. hobby + -es = *hobbies.*

3. baby + -es = ~~babies.~~ *babies.*

4. puppy + -es = *puppies.*

5. cry + -ed = *cried*

6. hurry + -ed = *hurried*

7. dry + -ed = *dried*

8. copy + -ed = *copied.*

Copy each sentence. Add *-es* or *-ed* to the underlined word.

9. Three <u>family</u> came to the school.

_____

10. We have <u>try</u> to eat less fat and more fruit.

_____

11. The worker had <u>hurry</u> to the bus stop.

_____

12. Make seven <u>copy</u> of the page.

copies

13. The storms were followed by blue <u>sky</u>.

skies

14. The wet towels <u>dry</u> in the warm sun yesterday.

dried.

Score: /14

ⓓ Proofread and Write

Shantel wrote this plan for better eating. She made **three** spelling mistakes. She also made a mistake when adding -*es* to a word. Cross out the misspelled words. Write the correct spellings above them.

Plan for Better Eating

- Try to eat more things from the bread category.

- Eat less from the meat and fats category~~es~~. ~~Yes~~

- Start each day with ~~cereel~~ *cereal* and a banana.

- Put nothing sweet in my ~~stumach~~ *stomach* after dinner.

- Use skim milk ~~insted~~ *instead* of whole milk.

- Have fruit for lunch more often.

Write your plan for better eating. Use at least three list words.

_____

_____

_____

_____

_____

_____

Writing Portfolio

Proofread your plan carefully and correct any mistakes. Then make a clean copy and put it in your writing portfolio.

Unit 2 Review

Finish the Meaning

Fill in the circle next to the word that best completes each sentence.

1. The _____ storm lasted only a few minutes.

   Ⓐ sweet   Ⓒ cautious
   Ⓑ peculiar   Ⓓ brief

2. Ice cream _____ a lot of fat. Do not eat it too often.

   Ⓐ receives   Ⓒ repeats
   Ⓑ contains   Ⓓ recovers

3. Fresh _____ is good for you.

   Ⓐ fruit   Ⓒ flour
   Ⓑ eyes   Ⓓ butter

4. Always protect your _____ when going outside in the sun.

   Ⓐ neighbor   Ⓒ skin
   Ⓑ machine   Ⓓ finger

5. The workers were in _____ of losing their jobs.

   Ⓐ style   Ⓒ peril
   Ⓑ support   Ⓓ choice

6. After his long run, Jerry felt dizzy and _____.

   Ⓐ brief   Ⓒ unfamiliar
   Ⓑ enough   Ⓓ weak

7. Kim always rides her _____ to work.

   Ⓐ bicycle   Ⓒ collar
   Ⓑ clinic   Ⓓ lease

8. Firefighters know how to _____ people from burning buildings.

   Ⓐ wrinkle   Ⓒ rescue
   Ⓑ contain   Ⓓ vibrate

9. Listen carefully. I do not want to _____ what I am saying.

   Ⓐ burn   Ⓒ shrink
   Ⓑ repeat   Ⓓ bounce

10. Is skydiving really worth the _____?

    Ⓐ risk   Ⓒ temperature
    Ⓑ guess   Ⓓ height

11. I'm not sure _____ Joe is coming.

    Ⓐ another   Ⓒ whether
    Ⓑ instead   Ⓓ already

12. We took Latoya to the hospital because she had a bad _____ on her leg.

    Ⓐ clinic   Ⓒ bicycle
    Ⓑ burn   Ⓓ peril

GO ON ▶

Check the Spelling

Fill in the circle next to the word that is spelled correctly and best completes each sentence.

13. The hot soup will burn your _____.

- (A) tunge
- (B) tongue ✓
- (C) tonge
- (D) tungue

14. Ken has a _____ of talking too loud.

- (A) habet
- (B) habbit
- (C) habit
- (D) habitt

15. Oats are a very healthy _____ to eat.

- (A) grane
- (B) grayne
- (C) graine
- (D) grain

16. If you need help, ask someone to _____ you.

- (A) assist
- (B) asist
- (C) assiste
- (D) assest

17. Ted _____ the fly ball and won the game.

- (A) cawght
- (B) caugt
- (C) caught
- (D) cawt

18. Every morning we have hot or cold _____ for breakfast.

- (A) cerel
- (B) cerelle
- (C) ceryul
- (D) cereal

19. Make sure the water is not too hot when you _____ the baby.

- (A) bath
- (B) bathe ✓
- (C) baythe
- (D) baith

20. The fire was a great _____ to the town.

- (A) tragedy
- (B) trajedy
- (C) trajady
- (D) tragedie

21. We had heard the song before. It was a _____ tune.

- (A) familer
- (B) familear
- (C) familliar
- (D) familiar

22. To open the bottle, _____ and turn the lid.

- (A) squeze
- (B) squeeze
- (C) skweeze
- (D) skueaze

23. The kitchen must be kept _____.

- (A) cleen
- (B) clene
- (C) clean
- (D) kleen

24. The cut on her _____ will heal soon.

- (A) knee
- (B) nee
- (C) knea
- (D) kneegh

STOP

Getting the Job You Want

(A) Check the Meaning

Read the paragraph below. Think about the meaning of the words in bold type.

The best job is a job you enjoy doing. If you like to **cook**, look for work at a school or hospital. There are also other places that need cooks. A large **employer** of workers will have a **cafeteria**. There the workers can get hot food for lunch. Some people like to stay **active** and do not mind hard **labor**. If you are one of them, **apply** for work in a storeroom or at a loading dock. If you like to **paint**, talk to some painters. Houses must be painted when it is warm. Extra help is often needed. However, when you get the job, set your alarm **clock**. You don't want to **arrive** for work late.

Write each word in bold type next to its meaning. Check your answers in the Mini-Dictionary.

Apply   **1.** to ask for a job

Arrive   **2.** to get to a place

School   **3.** a place for teaching and learning

Cook   **4.** to make food ready for eating

Employer   **5.** someone who pays people for work

Clock   **6.** something that shows the time of day

Active   **7.** able to act, work, or move

Cafeteria   **8.** a place to eat where food is bought at a counter

labor   **9.** work

Paint   **10.** to cover or coat with a liquid color

B Study the Spelling

Word List				
cook	apply	arrive	school	clock
employer	active	cafeteria	labor	paint

Write the list word or words for each clue.

1. They have a double consonant in their spelling.

   Apply   _Arrive._

2. They have a double vowel in their spelling.

   Cook   _School._

3. It comes from the word *employ*. _employer_

4. The word *act* is part of its spelling. _active._

5. It begins with *cl* and rhymes with *dock*. _clock._

6. The word *cafe* is part of its spelling. _Cafeteria._

7. It rhymes with *neighbor*. _~~cook~~ Labor._

8. They have one syllable and five letters.

   clock   _~~Arrive~~ Paint._

Write the list words with two syllables. Use dots between the syllables.

9. _labor_   11. _Apply_

10. _____   12. _Arrive_

Add the missing syllable. Write the list word.

13. cafe _te_ ria _Cafeteria._

14. em _ploy_ er _employer._

15. _Ac_ tive. _Active._

16. _Ar_ rive _Arrive._

17. la _bor._ _Labor._

18. ap _ply_ _Apply._

Score: ☐/18

C Build Your Skills

Language Tutor

A suffix is an ending added to a word. A suffix changes the meaning of the word. The *-er* suffix adds the meaning "one who" to a word.

One who employs a person is an employer.

One who paints is a painter.

One who bakes is a baker.

Write the word with these meanings. Use the *-er* suffix.

1. One who helps _____

2. One who camps _____

3. One who sings _____

4. One who writes _____

5. One who fights _____

6. One who skates _____

7. One who heals _____

Write these sentences. Use a word with an *-er* suffix in place of the underlined words.

8. The <u>one who teaches</u> helped me write the paper.

_____

9. The <u>one who pitches</u> threw the ball.

_____

10. Listen quietly to the <u>one who speaks</u>.

_____

11.. The <u>one who farms</u> grows corn and oats.

_____

12. The <u>one who leads cheers</u> is wearing a uniform.

_____

D Proofread and Write

Gene saw a help-wanted ad and wrote this letter. He made three spelling mistakes. Cross out the misspelled words. Write the correct spellings above them.

1122 East 4th Street

Yuma, AZ 85365

September 2, 1997

Personnel Director

Handy Helpers, Inc.

449 Maple Court

Yuma, AZ 85365

Dear Sir or Madam:

I saw your ad in the paper. I want to apply for the job of general helper. I have worked in a cafetiria as a cook. I can paint and do all kinds of laber. I go to school in the morning, but I could arive ready for work by noon. If you give me a chance, you will find that I am a good worker.

Sincerely,

Gene Lester

Gene Lester

Writing Portfolio

On another piece of paper, write a letter to apply for a job. It can be a job you find in the newspaper or a job you would like to have some day. Use at least three list words.

Proofread your letter and correct any mistakes. Then make a clean copy. You can mail your letter or put it in your writing portfolio.

Getting Ahead

Ⓐ Check the Meaning

Read the paragraph below. Think about the meaning of the words in bold type.

Once a year, most workers are told how well they **perform** on their jobs. The **usual** way of doing this is with a written **report**. This is a big **event**. It could mean a pay raise or a lost job. It is not always **easy** to get a good report. Some jobs require that work be done by a certain time. If you are **late** and miss a **deadline**, you will not get a good report. An order that is not filled on time can **cost** the company money. An employer also expects workers to be on the job. Workers who are **absent** often cannot be counted on. Do not be afraid to ask if you are doing a good job. Sometimes it helps to sit down with your boss. Write down some job goals. **Agree** to meet in a month or two to see how well you are meeting your goals.

Write each word in bold type next to its meaning. Check your answers in the Mini-Dictionary.

_____ **1.** the day or time when something must be done

_____ **2.** to cause to suffer or to lose money

_____ **3.** not present; not where one should be

_____ **4.** happening often; common

_____ **5.** to do or fulfill

_____ **6.** something that happens

_____ **7.** a statement or description

_____ **8.** not hard or difficult

_____ **9.** to be of the same mind or opinion

_____ **10.** coming after the time it was needed

Score: ⁄10

B Study the Spelling

Word List

absent	perform	report	cost	easy
agree	event	deadline	late	usual

Add the missing letters. Write the list word.

1. abs____nt _____

2. us____ ____l _____

3. p____rf____rm _____

4. ea____y _____

5. de____dl____ne _____

6. ____v____nt _____

Write the list word for each clue.

7. It is made from two shorter words. _____

8. It has one syllable and one vowel. _____

9. The word *sent* is part of its spelling. _____

10. It rhymes with *gate*. _____

11. It has five letters and two vowels. _____

12. Change two letters in *depart* to make this word. _____

Write the list word that comes between these words in a dictionary.

13. acorn _____ amount

14. rail _____ tack

15. elbow _____ exact

16. team _____ walk

17. open _____ quick

18. blue _____ daily

Score: ____/18

C Build Your Skills

Language Tutor

A prefix is a word part put at the beginning of a word. It changes the meaning of the word.

The prefix *un-* adds the meaning "not" to a word.

The prefix *re-* adds the meaning "back" or "again" to a word.

un- + usual = unusual, meaning "not usual"

re- + write = rewrite, meaning "write again"

Add the prefix to the word. Write a new word.

1. re- + do =

_____

2. un- + wanted =

_____

3. un- + fair =

_____

4. re- + wrap =

_____

5. re- + paint =

_____

6. un- + even =

_____

7. re- + build =

_____

8. un- + happy =

_____

9. re- + pack =

_____

10. un- + pack =

_____

11. re- + order =

_____

12. un- + wind =

_____

Add the prefix *re-* or *un-* to the word in parentheses. Then write the sentences.

13. Our order was lost. I will have to _____ the book. (order)

_____

14. Joe was not paid for the work. He is an _____ worker. (paid)

_____

15. Marie spilled the milk. She had to _____ her glass. (fill)

_____

Ⓓ Proofread and Write

Kwan wrote this memo to his new boss. He wanted to meet with her to talk about his job. He made three spelling mistakes. Cross out the misspelled words. Write the correct spellings above them.

MEMO

Date: 8/4/98
To: Kim Lee
From: Kwan Chin
Subject: My Work

Could we agree to meet sometime this week? I want to preform my new job well, so I need to be sure about a few things.

- I think I know an eazy way to keep the cost down. Can we talk about it?

- What is the usuel way of cleaning the tools?

- What is the deadline for my report?

- If I must be late or absent, whom do I call?

Let me know a good time to meet. Maybe we can meet every month to be sure I am doing a good job for you.

Writing Portfolio

Write a memo to your boss or to someone you would like to work for. Use your own paper. Ask to meet to discuss your work. Use at least three list words.

Proofread your memo carefully. Correct any mistakes. Then make a clean copy. Send it to your boss or put it in your writing portfolio.

Job Safety

Ⓐ Check the Meaning

Read the safety rules below. Think about the meaning of the words in bold type.

West End Products, Inc.
Safety Rules

1. Workers must **always** wear **goggles** when using power tools. A small piece of wood or metal can put out an eye.

2. Do not smoke in the shop. One **careless** match could cause a fire.

3. Loose clothes are a **danger** around motors. **Because** of this, everyone must wear work clothes.

4. In case of fire, break the glass on the alarm box. Pull the **handle** on the alarm **toward** you.

5. Any safety ideas should be written down and **brought** to the office.

Last year we **almost** had a **perfect** safety record. This year we want everyone to be safe.

Write each word in bold type next to its meaning. Check your answers in the Mini-Dictionary.

because	**1.** for this reason; since
brought	**2.** past tense of *bring*, meaning "to take or carry"
almost	**3.** nearly, but not quite
goggles	**4.** glasses worn to guard the eyes
handle	**5.** part of a tool or door that is made to be held
danger	**6.** something that can cause harm
toward	**7.** in the direction of
always	**8.** every time
perfect	**9.** without mistakes or faults
careless	**10.** done without thought or care

Score: ⬜ / 10

B Study the Spelling

Word List

because	goggles	handle	brought	always
careless	almost	perfect	toward	danger

Form a list word by matching the beginning of a word in the first column with its ending in the second column. Write the list word.

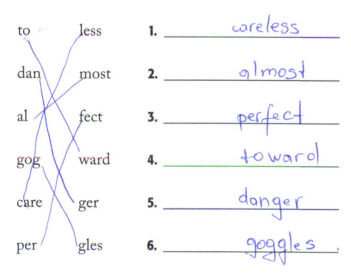

to less	1. _careless_
dan most	2. _almost_
al fect	3. _perfect_
gog ward	4. _toward_
care ger	5. _danger_
per gles	6. _goggles_

Write the list word or words for each clue.

7. The *gh* is silent in this word. ___brought___

8. The word *way* is part of its spelling. ___always___

9. It is plural. ___goggles___

10. The word *hand* is part of its spelling. ___handle___

11. This list word comes last in alphabetical order. ___toward___

12. The word *cause* is part of its spelling. ___because___

13. It ends with a double consonant. ___careless___

14. They begin with the same two letters.

___almost___   ___always___

15. It rhymes with *candle*. ___handle___

16. It begins like *day* and ends like *stranger*. ___danger___

Score: ☐ / 16

C Build Your Skills

Language Tutor

The suffix *-less* adds the meaning "without" to a word.

The suffix *-ful* adds the meaning "full of" to a word.

care + -less = careless, meaning "without care."

care + -ful = careful, meaning "full of care."

The suffixes *-less* and *-ful* change a word from a naming word to a describing word.

Naming Word	Good *care* is important for children.
Describing Word	Fred is a *careless* worker.
	Juan is a *careful* worker.

Add the suffix to the word. Write the new word.

1. use + -less =
   useless

2. use + -ful =
   useful

3. hope + -less =
   hopeless

4. hope + -ful =
   hopeful

5. thank + -ful =
   thankful

6. doubt + -less =
   doubtless

7. truth + -ful =
   truthful

8. end + -less =
   endless

9. flavor + -less =
   flavorless

10. fear + -ful =
    fearful

Write each sentence. Replace the underlined words with a word that has a *-ful* or *-less* suffix.

11. The prancing horses were <u>full of grace</u>.

    The prancing horses were graceful

12. The matches were <u>without use</u> after they got wet.

    The matches were useless after they got wet

D Proofread and Write

Hilary goes over this checklist before locking up at night. The list has three spelling mistakes. Cross out the misspelled words. Write the correct spellings above them.

FINAL CHECKLIST

❑ Always be sure doors are locked. The keys must be brought to the guard.

❑ ~~Gogles~~ *goggles* and tools must be put away.

❑ Be sure a ~~carless~~ *careless* driver has not left a motor running.

❑ Check the handle of the fire alarm. It must be ready for use.

❑ Turn the heat down to ~~allmost~~ *almost* sixty degrees.

❑ Report any signs of danger to the guard.

Writing Portfolio

Write a checklist you might use in your job or at home. Use your own paper. Use at least three list words.

Proofread your checklist carefully. Correct any mistakes. Then make a clean copy and put it in your writing portfolio.

The Worker's Handbook

A Check the Meaning

Read the paragraph below. Think about the meaning of the words in bold type.

Most employers give new workers a **handbook**. This book is **among** the most important books workers will ever have. It tells when the office or shop is open. It may not tell workers what they will **earn**, **although** they should find this in a contract or a letter. A good handbook also explains rules for taking time off. **Perhaps** the rules will **allow** one **week** of time off after six months on the job. The handbook should also explain the overtime plan. For example, someone working on Sunday may get **double** pay. If so, **people** who work on that day may get $24 per hour instead of $12 per hour. The handbook also will list other **rewards** that employers give workers. Some employers give health insurance. Others pay to send workers to school. Workers need to know all these things. This is why a handbook is an important tool.

Write each word in bold type next to its meaning. Check your answers in the Mini-Dictionary.

_____week._____ **1.** seven days in a row, usually from Sunday to Saturday

_____double_____ **2.** two times as much

_____earn_____ **3.** to get something for working

_____handbook_____ **4.** a book of facts or information that can be checked easily

_____although._____ **5.** even though; in spite of the fact

_____reward_____ **6.** gifts or prizes given in return for good service

_____allow_____ **7.** to let happen; to permit

_____perhaps_____ **8.** maybe; possibly

_____among_____ **9.** in the middle of, surrounded by

_____people_____ **10.** persons; men, women, and children

B Study the Spelling

Word List				
people	double	allow	handbook	reward
although	earn	perhaps	among	week

Write the list word or words for each clue.

1. It has a double consonant in its spelling. _____

2. The final *gh* is silent. _____

3. It is made from two words. _____

4. They end with *le*. _____ _____

5. They have a double vowel in their spelling.

   _____ _____

6. They have just one syllable. _____ _____

7. They begin with *al*. _____ _____

8. It rhymes with *trouble*. _____

Add the missing letters. Write the list word.

9. r_e_w_a_rd

   _____

10. _a_m_o_ng

    _____

11. per_h_ _a_ps

    _____

12. ___ ___rn

    _____

13. do___b___e

    _____

14. pe___p___e

    _____

One word in each group is misspelled. Circle the misspelled word. Write it correctly.

15. prehaps   people   week   _____

16. although   allow   amung   _____

17. earn   double   hanbook   _____

18. rewerd   although   people   _____

ⓒ Build Your Skills

Language Tutor

A compound word is a word made from two shorter words.

hand + book = handbook   sun + shine = sunshine

mean + while = meanwhile   out + side = outside

Put these words together. Write a compound word.

1. may + be =

maybe

2. no + body =

nobody

3. with + out =

without

4. foot + ball =

football

5. birth + day =

birthday

6. grand + mother =

grandmother

7. home + sick =

homesick

8. for + ever =

forever

9. bed + room =

bedroom

10. rail + road =

railroad

11. day + light =

daylight

12. every + thing =

everything

Add the missing word to make a compound word. Then copy the complete sentence.

13. Put on your coat before going out_side ._____.

_____

14. After a week at camp, she became _____home____sick.

_____

15. We waited for thirty minutes, but it seemed like for_ever_____.

_____

Score: ╱ 15

ⓓ Proofread and Write

Kate has a new job. She made this list of things to do on her first day. Kate made three spelling mistakes. Cross out the misspelled words. Write the correct spellings above them.

Things to Do

Be among the first people to get to work.

Find out which days I work next ~~weak~~ week.

See if I can earn extra money by working late.

Study the handbook. ~~Purhaps~~ Perhaps find ways of getting added rewards.

Find out if they allow time off to go to school.

Ask about working a ~~doubel~~ double shift.

Make a list of things you would want to do if you started a new job. Use at least three list words.

_____

_____

_____

_____

Writing Portfolio

Proofread your list carefully and correct any mistakes. Then make a clean copy and put it in your writing portfolio.

Unit 3 Review

Finish the Meaning

Fill in the circle next to the word that best completes each sentence.

1. Everyone passed. It was a(n) _____ test.

   Ⓐ active Ⓒ cautious
   Ⓑ easy Ⓓ peculiar

2. Each worker gets a _____. It tells how to work the machines.

   Ⓐ clock Ⓒ handbook
   Ⓑ lease Ⓓ collar

3. Be safe on the job! Don't be a _____ worker.

   Ⓐ careless Ⓒ perfect
   Ⓑ familiar Ⓓ peculiar

4. I cannot spend that much for eggs. They _____ too much.

   Ⓐ bounce Ⓒ cost
   Ⓑ repeat Ⓓ allow

5. The _____ said that we are doing much better than last year.

   Ⓐ report Ⓒ handle
   Ⓑ support Ⓓ peril

6. Joe and Kip will _____ a big meal for the team.

   Ⓐ rescue Ⓒ earn
   Ⓑ cook Ⓓ bounce

7. All the workers _____ that the boss is fair.

   Ⓐ agree Ⓒ determine
   Ⓑ move Ⓓ smell

8. Many of us work at the auto plant. It is the biggest _____ in town.

   Ⓐ house Ⓒ neighbor
   Ⓑ family Ⓓ employer

9. After we _____ the room, the house will look much better.

   Ⓐ allow Ⓒ report
   Ⓑ paint Ⓓ cost

10. Sandy watched the _____. She wanted to be on time.

    Ⓐ cost Ⓒ labor
    Ⓑ clock Ⓓ quart

11. Tim is here every day. He is never _____.

    Ⓐ unfamiliar Ⓒ absent
    Ⓑ family Ⓓ fruit

12. Safety _____ must be worn in the metal shop.

    Ⓐ fruit Ⓒ dollars
    Ⓑ events Ⓓ goggles

GO ON ▶

Check the Spelling

Fill in the circle next to the word that is spelled correctly and best completes each sentence.

13. The _____ year runs from September to June.

  (A) skool   (C) schul
  (B) school   (D) schule

14. Every _____ we go to a safety workshop.

  (A) weke   (C) wek
  (B) weak   (D) week

15. There is always a big _____ of fire at the wood mill.

  (A) danjer   (C) dangur
  (B) danjur   (D) danger

16. We all worked extra hard to meet the _____.

  (A) deadline (C) deadlyne
  (B) dedline   (D) deadlion

17. Ten _____ offered to help us move.

  (A) peeple   (C) people
  (B) peaple   (D) peopel

18. Helen _____ us oranges from Florida.

  (A) brot   (C) brout
  (B) brought (D) brawght

19. Each day the _____ serves lunch to 350 people.

  (A) cafateria (C) cafeteria
  (B) cafiteria (D) kafeteria

20. The train was moving _____ us at great speed.

  (A) taurd   (C) taward
  (B) toword (D) toward

21. If I miss the bus, I will be _____ for work.

  (A) layte   (C) late
  (B) lait   (D) lat

22. Bob found the lost file. It was _____ the old tools.

  (A) amung   (C) among
  (B) emong   (D) ahmong

23. People who _____ well get good job reviews.

  (A) perform (C) perfurm
  (B) preform (D) praform

24. Julio offered a _____ for the lost ring.

  (A) reword   (C) rewourd
  (B) reeward (D) reward

STOP

Score: _____ / 24

Summer Fun

Ⓐ Check the Meaning

Read the paragraph below. Think about the meaning of the words in bold type.

The **summer** can be **either** a happy time or a sad time. School is out. The days are warm and sunny. Even so, a **parent** hears **children** moan, "There's nothing to do." You may **doubt** there is much you can do about this. It takes money to send a child to **camp**. Spending money is not always needed, however. There are things children can do that cost little or nothing. You need to know where to look. Some towns have a lake with a **beach**. It costs nothing to use it. In some parks, the city forms teams to play baseball or soccer. The winners **often** get prizes they can be **proud** of all year. The town **library** may have a free story hour. Churches sometimes offer picnics and trips at no cost. The town and the church are good places to find free things to do.

Write each word in bold type next to its meaning. Check your answers in the Mini-Dictionary.

_____parent_____ **1.** a father or mother

_____doubt_____ **2.** to be unsure about something

_____library_____ **3.** a place where books, other reading items, and films are kept

_____often_____ **4.** happening many times

_____camp._____ **5.** an outside area with tents or cabins used for fun

_____children_____ **6.** the plural of *child*; two or more young girls or boys

_____either_____ **7.** one or the other

_____proud_____ **8.** feeling good about something

_____summer_____ **9.** the season of the year that comes after spring

_____beach._____ **10.** a sandy area of land next to a body of water

B Study the Spelling

Word List

parent	doubt	library	often	camp
children	either	proud	summer	beach

Add the missing letters. Write the words.

1. lib_r_ a _r_ y ___library___

2. of_t_ _e_ n ___often___

3. e_i_ th_e_ r ___either___

4. sum_m_ _e_ r ___summer___

5. chi_l_ dr_e_ n ___children___

6. p_a_ r _e_ nt ___parent___

7. pr_o_ _u_ d ___proud___

Write the list word or words for each clue.

8. They have one syllable ___beach___ ___camp___
___doubt___ ___proud___

9. It rhymes with *peach*. ___beach___

10. It has a silent *b* in its spelling. ___doubt___

11. They end with *er*. ___either___ ___summer___

12. They end with *en*. ___children___ ___often___

13. It has three syllables. ___library___

14. They have a vowel sound spelled *ou*.
___doubt___ ___proud___

15. It has a double consonant in its spelling. ___summer___

16. It rhymes with *lamp*. ___camp___

Write the list words that begin with two consonants. Underline the vowels.

17. ___children___

18. ___proud___

Score: [X] 18

C Build Your Skills

Language Tutor

Most words form their plural by adding *-s* or *-es*. Some words form their plurals in unusual ways. These unusual plurals must be remembered.

Singular	Plural	Singular	Plural
child	children	foot	feet
man	men	woman	women
tooth	teeth	mouse	mice
goose	geese	ox	oxen

Write the sentence or sentences. Add the singular or plural form of the underlined word.

1. The <u>man</u> called a meeting. Many _____ men _____ were there.

The man called a meeting. Many men were there

2. The <u>mice</u> were in a cage. One _____ mouse _____ was white.

The mice were in a cage. One mouse was white

3. Except for one _____ tooth _____, all her <u>teeth</u> were fine.

Except for one tooth, all her teeth were fine.

4. Everyone's <u>feet</u> hurt. My left _____ foot _____ was very sore.

Everyone's feet hurt. My left foot was very sore

5. One <u>child</u> is missing. There should be five _____ children _____ here.

One child is missing. There should be five children here

6. We studied many great <u>women</u>. One _____ woman _____, Mother Teresa, stood out.

We studied many great women. One woman, Mother Teresa stood o

7. One <u>goose</u> escaped. We still had four _____ geese _____ left.

One goose escaped. We still had four geese left.

8. An <u>ox</u> took a day to do the work. Four _____ oxen _____ did it in an hour.

An ox took a day to do the work. Four oxen did it in an hour

ⓓ Proofread and Write

Paula has made this plan for school vacation. She made three spelling mistakes. Cross out the misspelled words. Write the correct spellings above them.

SUMMER PLANS.
~~SUMER~~ PLANS

- Take the children to the beach often.
  I doubt that it will be crowded.

- Join the Parent Club at school.

- Plan either ~~eithur~~ a weekend at camp or a
  day in the city.

- Find out if the library ~~libary~~ has a program.
  I would be proud if Tina read lots of
  books this summer.

Write a plan for things to do in the summer. Use at least three list words.

_____

_____

_____

_____

Writing Portfolio

Proofread your plan carefully and correct any mistakes. Then make a clean copy and put it in your writing portfolio.

Sending Mail

Ⓐ Check the Meaning

Read the paragraph below. Think about the meaning of the words in bold type.

Some things we send must arrive on time. A birthday **package** and an **answer** to a job ad are two such things. There are some things you can do to avoid a **delay**. Mail is picked up **daily** in most places. Know what time your **letter** carrier picks up your mail. Have your mail ready **early**. Besides the name, street, and **city**, you must also give the ZIP code. Having all the **necessary** information makes it easier for the post office to **deliver** mail on time. It is now possible to send things anywhere in the country in a day or less. This costs much more than **normal** first-class mail, which may take days. Today there are other ways to send messages. You can fax or E-mail a letter in minutes. Some people call the old way of mailing letters "snail mail."

Write each word in bold type next to its meaning. Check your answers in the Mini-Dictionary.

letter	**1.** a written message
daily	**2.** happening every day
normal	**3.** usual or regular
delay	**4.** lateness
answer	**5.** a reply to a question
necessary	**6.** needed
city	**7.** a place where many people live and work
package	**8.** a box or case with one or more things packed inside
early	**9.** happening before the usual time
deliver	**10.** to take to a person or place

Score: ___ / 10

B Study the Spelling

Word List

delay	letter	early	city	normal
package	answer	daily	deliver	necessary

Add the missing syllable. Write a list word.

1. cit_y_ _____city_____

2. __let__ ter _____letter_____

3. __an__ swer _____answer_____

4. __de__ lay _____delay_____

Write the list word or words for each clue.

5. They have a double consonant in their spelling.

_____delay_____ _____daily_____

6. It has three syllables. _____deliver_____

7. They end with *ly*. _____early_____ _____daily_____

8. It has four letters and two syllables. _____city_____

9. It has four syllables. _____necessary_____

10. It has a silent *w* in its spelling. _____answer_____

Write the three words that begin with *d* in alphabetical order.

11. _____delay_____

12. _____daily_____

13. _____deliver_____

One word in each group is misspelled. Circle the misspelled word. Write it correctly.

14. necesary   delay   city   _____necesary_____

15. packege   deliver   daily   _____package_____

16. city   normel   letter   _____normal_____

Language Tutor

An envelope needs to give information. This way the post office can move it more quickly. Study the envelope below.

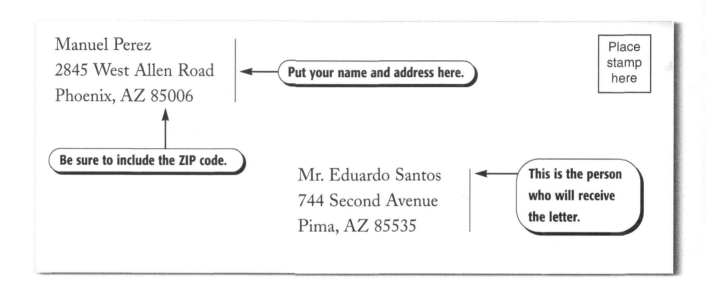

Manuel Perez
2845 West Allen Road
Phoenix, AZ 85006

Put your name and address here.

Be sure to include the ZIP code.

Place stamp here

Mr. Eduardo Santos
744 Second Avenue
Pima, AZ 85535

This is the person who will receive the letter.

Study the envelope. Answer these questions.

1. Who sent this letter? _This letter sent Manuel Perez_

2. What is the sender's street address? _The sender's street address is 2845 West Allen Road_

3. In what town does the sender live? _The sender lives in Phoenix_

4. What is the sender's ZIP code? _The sender's ZIP code is 85006_

5. Who will receive the letter? _The letter will receive Mr. Eduardo Santos_

6. What is his street address? _His street address is 744 Second Avenue_

7. In what town does he live? _He lives in Pimo_

8. What is his ZIP code? _His ZIP code is 85535_

9. Are capital letters used at the beginnings of names of people, streets, and towns?
   Yes, they are capital letters.

10. What goes in the upper right-hand corner? _Place stamp._

D Proofread and Write

Eduardo wrote this letter to his sister. He made three spelling mistakes. Cross out the misspelled words. Write the correct spellings above them.

744 Second Avenue

Pima, AZ 85536

April 17, 1997

Dear Gloria,

I am sorry I forgot your birthday. It is not normal for me to

forget it. I was out of the city and too busy to check the date.

I sent a ~~pakage~~ *package* last night. It should be ~~dalivered~~ *delivered* by the

time this letter arrives. With luck, it will get there ~~earley~~ *early*.

Next year I will do better. I will do what is necessary to

keep this day in mind. Please forgive me this year.

Your brother,

Eduardo

Writing Portfolio

Write a friendly letter to someone. Prepare an envelope for your letter. Use your own paper and envelope. Use at least three list words.

Proofread your letter and envelope carefully. Correct any mistakes. Then make a clean copy to mail or to put in your writing portfolio.

The School and the Home

Ⓐ Check the Meaning

Read the paragraph below. Think about the meaning of the words in bold type.

We all want our children to **achieve** good marks in school. There are many ways you can help. **Visit** your child's school and meet the teacher. Do not wait until there is a **problem**. This meeting is a good time to ask a **question** about the class. How is my child doing? Are there things we can do at home? Will there will be **homework** to do every night? Know which **book** is used for each **course**. **Whenever** there is homework, be sure your child brings home the right book. You cannot **study** math at home if the book is still at school. Find a quiet place where your child can work. Teach your child to plan ahead. If a report is due on Monday, do not wait until **noon** on Sunday to start. Talk about what happens in school every day. Children do better when they know the family cares.

Write each word in bold type next to its meaning. Check your answers in the Mini-Dictionary.

homework	**1.** work done at home
course	**2.** a class in school; subject
achieve	**3.** to meet a goal
problem	**4.** a difficulty
book	**5.** a set of pages with written information that is held together
study	**6.** to try to learn
visit	**7.** to go to see
whenever	**8.** at whatever time
noon	**9.** the middle of the day, lunch time
question	**10.** something that is asked

B Study the Spelling

Word List

problem ✓	homework ✓	question	book	achieve
course	study	visit	whenever	noon

Write the list word or words for each clue.

1. They have a double *o* in their spelling.

   book   noon

2. They are made from two smaller words.

   homework   whenever

3. They end with *on*. question   noon

4. It rhymes with *believe*. achieve

5. It begins like *stump* and ends like *lady*. study

Add the missing letters. Write the word.

6. prob_l_ _e_m   problem

7. c_o_ur_s_e   course

8. v_i_s_i_t   visit

9. qu_e_s_t_ion   question

10. st_u_d_y_   study

Write the list word that fits each shape.

11. book

13.  course

12.  achieve

14.  visit

C Build Your Skills

Language Tutor

Words spelled with *ie* or *ei* can be tricky. The rule that begins, "*i* before *e* except after *c* . . ." does not always work. Study these spellings:

achieve	pie	tie	ceiling
science	eight	belief	niece
review	thief	chief	receive
die	seize	yield	neither

Add *ie* or *ei*. Write the word.

1. e i ght
   eight

2. th i e f
   thief

3. rev i e w
   review

4. d i e
   die

5. ch i e f
   chief

6. n e i ther
   neither

7. c e i ling
   ceiling

8. sc i e nce
   science

9. n i e ce
   niece

10. bel i e f
    bilief

11. p i e
    pie

12. y i e ld
    yield

13. ach i e ve
    achieve

14. t i e
    tie

15. rec e i ve
    raceive

16. s e i ze
    seize

Score: /16

Ⓓ Proofread and Write

Yolanda made this list of things to ask her son's teacher. She made three spelling mistakes. Cross out the misspelled words. Write the correct spellings above them.

Things to Ask Sammy's Teacher

- Can I ~~visut~~ *visit* the class some time?

- Is noon a good time to come?

- We sometimes have a question about

  the ~~homewerk~~ *homework*. Is it all right to call you

  at home?

- Does Sammy have time to study at

  school?

- How can Sammy ~~acheive~~ *achieve* better grades

  in math?

- Can we get a book to explain the math

  problem?

Writing Portfolio

Write a list of questions to ask your teacher or your child's teacher. Use your own paper. Use at least three list words.

Proofread your questions carefully and correct any mistakes. Then make a clean copy and put it in your writing portfolio.

16 Planning a Trip

Ⓐ Check the Meaning

Read the paragraph below. Think about the meaning of the words in bold type.

There are many ways to **travel**. Flying is the quickest way. Planes will speed you **above** the clouds from city to city. A **train** takes longer, but it costs less. To many, however, driving is best. Drivers, of course, run the risk of getting lost. One **mistake** and you can go miles out of your way. After bringing your **license** to drive, a good map is the most **important** thing to take along. Find where you want to go. Draw a **circle** around each of the places you want to see on the way. Then find the road or **highway** that gets you from place to place. If you have time, try some small **country** roads. Many maps will mark a pretty area, like a covered **bridge** over a stream. Enjoy the trip. There is more to travel than just getting there.

Write each word in bold type next to its meaning. Check your answers in the Mini-Dictionary.

Country   **1.** area away from the cities

travel   **2.** to go from place to place

mistake   **3.** something done in an incorrect way

highway   **4.** a large, paved road

bridge   **5.** a structure built over water or roads so people and cars can cross over

train   **6.** railroad cars pulled by an engine

above   **7.** at a higher level

important   **8.** of great worth or value

licese   **9.** a paper or card permitting you to do something

circle   **10.** a ring-like figure where all points are the same distance from the center

B Study the Spelling

Word List

train	circle	highway	important	country
bridge	license	above	travel	mistake

Write the list word for each clue.

1. There is a silent *d* in the spelling. _bridse_

2. The word *take* is part of its spelling. _mistake_

3. It has just one syllable and rhymes with *drain*. _train_

4. It rhymes with *one love*. _above_

5. It is made up of two smaller words. _highway_

6. It begins like *lice* and ends like *sense*. _license_

7. It ends with *el*. _travel_

8. It ends with *le*. _circle_

9. It has three syllables and ends with *ant*. _important_

10. Put a letter in *county* to make this word. _country_

Write the list words that begin with two consonants. Circle the word that comes last in alphabetical order.

11. _train_

12. _bridge_

13. _(fridge)_

Add the missing letters. Write the list word.

14. li_c_ en_s_ e _license_

15. imp_o_ rt_a_ nt _important_

16. c_i_ rc_l_ e _circle_

17. c_o_ unt_r_ y _country_

18. _a_ b_o_ ve _above_

Score: ___/18

C Build Your Skills

Language Tutor

We use the word *I* to stand for ourselves. It is always capitalized.

Jim and I rode the train to Memphis.

A sentence also begins with a capital letter.

Listen for an important call.

Copy each sentence. Use capital letters where they are needed.

1. this is an important test.

_____

2. never have i seen such trees.

_____

3. we drove above the cliff.

_____

4. now i know why you came.

_____

5. she drew a circle on the paper.

_____

6. will i be there on time?

_____

7. you must pay a toll on the bridge.

_____

8. if i make a mistake, you will know.

_____

9. this country road has many bumps.

_____

10. tammy and i have a license.

_____

Score: ___ / 10

Ⓓ Proofread and Write

Dave got this postcard from a friend on a trip. It has three spelling mistakes. The writer also forgot to use a capital letter. Cross out the misspelled words. Write the correct spellings above them. Add the missing capital letter.

June 27, 1997

Dear Dave,

This has been a great trip! This is the loveliest country I have ever seen. We had to take a boat to our campground. There is no brige over the stream. large birds fly in a cercle above our camp. Nothing important seems to happen here. I like that. I now have a license to fish. Hope I bring some fish home.

Your friend,

Miguel

Dave McDonald

732 Fort Sanders Rd.

Charlotte, NC 28210

Writing Portfolio

Write a postcard to a friend. Use your own paper. Tell about a place you visited or would like to visit. Use at least three list words.

Proofread your postcard carefully. Correct any mistakes. Then make a clean copy. You can mail your postcard or put it in your writing portfolio.

Unit 4 Review

Finish the Meaning

Fill in the circle next to the word that best completes each sentence.

1. John got a gift mailed in a _____ for his birthday.

   Ⓐ handle   Ⓒ package
   Ⓑ choice   Ⓓ category

2. You must have your _____ to drive a car.

   Ⓐ license   Ⓒ report
   Ⓑ goggles   Ⓓ reward

3. The storm pounded the shore. The town decided to close the _____.

   Ⓐ dairy   Ⓒ beach
   Ⓑ country   Ⓓ clinic

4. We got a friendly _____ from Uncle Henry. It came in today's mail.

   Ⓐ letter   Ⓒ delay
   Ⓑ handbook   Ⓓ lease

5. Always do your _____ right after class. Do not put it off until later.

   Ⓐ temperature   Ⓒ visit
   Ⓑ homework   Ⓓ license

6. Drive slowly around the park. Many young _____ ride their bikes there.

   Ⓐ employers   Ⓒ children
   Ⓑ bridges   Ⓓ schools

7. Get to the game _____. Seats are gone quickly.

   Ⓐ early   Ⓒ enough
   Ⓑ often   Ⓓ seldom

8. It took hours to drive here. The _____ was closed.

   Ⓐ camp   Ⓒ penny
   Ⓑ rescue   Ⓓ highway

9. I needed help from the teacher. I could not solve the _____.

   Ⓐ style   Ⓒ habit
   Ⓑ problem   Ⓓ city

10. It will be a difficult test. You must _____ hard.

    Ⓐ guess   Ⓒ shrink
    Ⓑ travel   Ⓓ study

11. The chair will not fit in the car. The store will have to _____ it.

    Ⓐ deliver   Ⓒ contain
    Ⓑ receive   Ⓓ double

12. You did a great job. Everyone is _____ of you.

    Ⓐ cautious   Ⓒ familiar
    Ⓑ proud   Ⓓ careless

GO ON ➤

Check the Spelling

Fill in the circle next to the word that is spelled correctly and best completes each sentence.

13. Taking the _____ to work will save time.

- (A) trane
- (B) trayne
- (C) train
- (D) trein

14. Go to the _____ if you need a book.

- (A) liberry
- (B) library
- (C) libary
- (D) liebrary

15. I have the _____ skills for this job.

- (A) necessary
- (B) nesessary
- (C) nesessary
- (D) necesary

16. A _____ on first aid can save your life.

- (A) corse
- (B) coarce
- (C) cource
- (D) course

17. Speak to _____ Tom or Bill. One of them will know.

- (A) eithre
- (B) either
- (C) eyether
- (D) eithur

18. We have an _____ deadline coming up.

- (A) impourtant
- (B) inportant
- (C) important
- (D) importent

19. A clear set of goals will help you _____ your dreams.

- (A) achieve
- (B) acheve
- (C) acheive
- (D) achive

20. We meet _____ to talk about the plans.

- (A) dayly
- (B) daily
- (C) daly
- (D) dailie

21. You will do a great job. I have no _____ about that.

- (A) dout
- (B) dowt
- (C) doubt
- (D) dought

22. Draw a _____ on the chalkboard.

- (A) sirkle
- (B) circel
- (C) cercle
- (D) circle

23. They will have an _____ for us by next week.

- (A) answer
- (B) anser
- (C) answre
- (D) ansir

24. There will be plenty of time for _____ later.

- (A) kwestions
- (B) questions
- (C) queschuns
- (D) questiuns

Score: _____ / 24

17 The Final Word

A Check the Meaning

Read the paragraph below. Think about the meaning of the words in bold type.

In the United States, the people have the **final** word. They decide who runs our towns and our nation when they **vote**. It all begins when people **declare** they will run for an **office**, such as mayor. Each person usually has a different **belief** about how to solve a problem. A group of people with the same beliefs may help someone running for office. This group is called a **party**. Each person running for office must make his or her beliefs known. This may be done with a **speech**, posters, or TV ads. **Victory** often goes to the one who can best sell his or her beliefs. One's vote should be based on **thorough** study. Only one person can win. The other must **lose**. The voter is the one in charge. He or she will decide.

Write each word in bold type next to its meaning. Check your answers in the Mini-Dictionary.

_____ **1.** a group of people taking one side in a contest

_____ **2.** to make a choice by casting a ballot

_____ **3.** complete

_____ **4.** an idea held to be true

_____ **5.** to fail to win

_____ **6.** the act of saying something with words

_____ **7.** the winning of a contest

_____ **8.** to state in a strong, formal way

_____ **9.** last

_____ **10.** a public post or position

Score: /10

B Study the Spelling

Word List

thorough	party	vote	belief	lose
speech	victory	declare	final	office

Write the list word or words for each clue.

1. It ends with a silent *gh*. _____

2. It has a double consonant in its spelling. _____

3. It has three syllables. _____

4. They begin and end with two consonants.

_____   _____

5. It contains the word *part* in its spelling. _____

6. There is an *ie* in its spelling. _____

7. It rhymes with *note*. _____

8. It starts like *decline* and ends like *square*. _____

9. They end with a vowel, consonant, and *e*. _____

_____   _____   _____

Add the missing syllable. Write the list word.

10. fi_____   _____

11. vic_____ry   _____

12. _____ty   _____

One word in each group is misspelled. Circle the misspelled word. Write it correctly.

13. office   thorough   luse   _____

14. belief   party   speach   _____

15. vote   fynal   victory   _____

16. declair   thorough   office   _____

C Build Your Skills

Every sentence ends with a punctuation mark.

A statement ends with a period.

The mayor gave a speech.

A question ends with a question mark.

Did you like what he said?

An exclamation of strong feelings ends with an exclamation point.

Run for your life!

Write these sentences. Add the final punctuation.

1. Four people are running for that office__

_____

2. Do you belong to a political party__

_____

3. What a great speech__

_____

4. It is your duty to vote__

_____

5. Has he been declared the winner__

_____

6. Did you do a thorough study of the problem__

_____

7. A victory party is planned for tonight__

_____

8. Look out__

_____

Score: /8

Ⓓ Proofread and Write

The posters below have three spelling mistakes. The final punctuation is wrong on one poster. Cross out the misspelled words and the incorrect punctuation. Write the correct spellings and the correct punctuation above them.

VOTE
for Smith.
His pardy cares.

Victory!
You can't lose with
Marge Tooze.

Do you want a change.

Vote for Sam LaPoint.

He's a man with a balief

in the future.

Have you heard
enough from others?

Listen to Sandy Baker tonight.

This is your finel chance to

hear her great speech.

Write some posters on the lines below. Use at least three list words.

_____

_____

_____

_____

_____

_____

Writing Portfolio

Proofread your posters carefully. Correct any mistakes. Then make clean copies and put them in your writing portfolio.

Traffic Tickets

Ⓐ Check the Meaning

Read the paragraph below. Think about the meaning of the words in bold type.

Many things are more **awful** than getting a **ticket**. It is not the worst **crime** you can commit. Still, seeing the flashing light of a **traffic** officer behind you can be scary. Do not become alarmed or **hostile**. It is wise to let the officer tell you what the problem is. If you get a ticket, do not gripe. The officer is not the **judge**. Most tickets for speeding carry a **fine**. You can usually just sign the ticket and pay the fine. If you become angry or swear, you may end up in **jail**. You can **choose** to deny you were speeding and **defend** yourself in court. You have the same rights for small crimes as you do for large ones.

Write each word in bold type next to its meaning. Check your answers in the Mini-Dictionary.

_____ **1.** to decide; to pick or select

_____ **2.** a slip of paper; a notice that you have broken the law

_____ **3.** an activity that is against the law

_____ **4.** money that someone who breaks the law must pay

_____ **5.** a person in charge of a court of law

_____ **6.** to speak for; to guard or protect

_____ **7.** openly and strongly unfriendly

_____ **8.** a place to hold prisoners or those waiting to be tried

_____ **9.** vehicles moving on the roads and streets

_____ **10.** very bad or unpleasant

Score: /10

B Study the Spelling

Word List

ticket	choose	jail	defend	judge
awful	fine	hostile	traffic	crime

Add the missing letters. Write the list word.

1. ch___ ___se _____

2. tra___ ___ic _____

3. a___ ___ul _____

4. d___f___nd _____

5. ju___ ___e _____

6. host___ ___e _____

7. cr___m___ _____

8. ti___k___t _____

Write the list word for each clue.

9. It has a silent *d* in its spelling. _____

10. There is a double consonant in its spelling. _____

11. Add the suffix *-ful* to *awe* to make this word. _____

12. Change one letter in *picket* to make this word. _____

13. Change the ending on *defense* to make this word. _____

14. It rhymes with *pail*. _____

15. The word *end* is part of its spelling. _____

Write the words with just one syllable. Circle the words that end with a vowel, consonant, and e.

16. _____   **19.** _____

17. _____   **20.** _____

18. _____

Score: ☐/20

C Build Your Skills

Language Tutor

Always capitalize a title and the name that follows it.

Mr. Samuel Parker   Ms. Juanita Rivera

Judge Marsha Jackson   Uncle Ken

Dr. W. D. Baxter   Captain Hudson

Do not capitalize a title following a name.

Marsha Jackson, the judge   Ken, my uncle

Wendy Baxter, the doctor   Frank Hudson, the captain

Write these sentences. Add capital letters where needed.

1. The case will be heard by judge wang.

_____

2. uncle Mark said we should see a doctor.

_____

3. An award was given to ms. amy rodman.

_____

4. Please rise when the judge enters.

_____

5. I need to see dr. wagner.

_____

6. If my sister has a baby, I will be an uncle.

_____

7. Is there a mr. simmons here?

_____

8. Take this message to captain dawson.

_____

Ⓓ Proofread and Write

Steve wrote this letter to a judge. He made three spelling mistakes. He also forgot to capitalize a word. Cross out the misspelled words. Write the correct spellings above them. Write the capital letter above where it should be.

378 Apple Lane

Elgin, NE 68636

November 2, 1997

The Honorable John R. Nelson

Judge of the County Court

High Point, NC 27261

Dear judge Nelson:

The police said I should write to you about my problem. I received a tiket in your county last week for driving too fast. I don't think I was going too fast. Other drivers in the traffic were going faster than I was. However, I cannot drive back to High Point to difend myself. I do not want to seem hostile, but this ticket is unfair. If I must, I will chose to pay the fine rather than go to jail. Please be fair in judging my situation. Let me know what your advice is.

Sincerely,

Steve Hanson

Steve Hanson

Writing Portfolio

Write a letter to a judge. Use your own paper. Ask about a ticket or get some information about the law. Use at least three list words.

Proofread your letter carefully and correct any mistakes. Then make a clean copy to mail or put in your writing portfolio.

The Civil War

Ⓐ Check the Meaning

Read the paragraph below. Think about the meaning of the words in bold type.

For four years, the United States was a divided nation. President Lincoln said we could not live **half** slave and half free. A bloody civil war would **prove** the **truth** of those words. The **world** watched as men fought one **battle** after another. Both sides showed **pride**. Both also held a deep **devotion** to **their** cause. In the end, the nation was able to **survive**. The cost was incredible. Seven thousand men were killed or hurt in one thirty-minute battle. The bloodiest day in U.S. history took place on a Maryland **field**. Sickness alone killed thousands. In all, more than 600,000 Americans were killed or wounded in the Civil War. This is more than all other U.S. wars put together.

Write each word in bold type next to its meaning. Check your answers in the Mini-Dictionary.

_____ **1.** a feeling of dignity or worth

_____ **2.** the Earth

_____ **3.** an area of land, usually open and clear

_____ **4.** a fight between two groups, usually with weapons

_____ **5.** something that is correct or true

_____ **6.** the possessive form of _they_; belonging to them

_____ **7.** to live through; to stay alive

_____ **8.** faithfulness; a loyal feeling

_____ **9.** being one of two equal parts

_____ **10.** to show something to be correct

B Study the Spelling

Word List

battle	half	pride	their	devotion
prove	field	survive	truth	world

Write the list word or words for each clue.

1. There is a silent *l* in its spelling. _____

2. Change two letters in *slide* to make this word. _____

3. It rhymes with *commotion*. _____

4. It has two syllables and a double consonant. _____

5. It rhymes with *shield*. _____

6. It has three syllables and ends with *tion*. _____

7. They end with *ld*. _____   _____

8. It rhymes with *air* but has no *a* in its spelling. _____

Write the list words with two or more syllables. Write them in alphabetical order.

9. _____   **11.** _____

10. _____

Write the list words that begin with two consonants. Circle the two that begin with the same consonants.

12. _____   **14.** _____

13. _____   **15.** _____

Write the list word that fits each shape.

16. [ ][ ][ ][ ][ ][ ]   **18.**

17.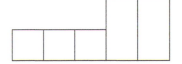

C Build Your Skills

Language Tutor

Some words sound alike, but they have different meanings and spellings. The underlined words sound alike, but they have different meanings and spellings.

their	belonging to them	This is <u>their</u> house.
there	a place	I want to go <u>there</u> some day.
	a word used to begin a sentence	<u>There</u> are fish in the water.
they're	they are	I know <u>they're</u> coming.
to	toward; in front of	Jim took a trip <u>to</u> Austin.
too	also	Can we come <u>too</u>?
	more than enough	The soup is <u>too</u> hot.
two	the number after one	They won by <u>two</u> points.

Study the meanings of the underlined words above. Then write the word in the parentheses that fits each sentence below.

1. The older boys came first. (To; Too; Two) girls also came. _____

2. The birds have built (their; there; they're) nests high in the trees. _____

3. No (to; too; two) snowflakes are alike. _____

4. I am not sure how to get (their; there; they're). _____

5. Keep going. We must get (to; too; two) Peoria today. _____

6. It will take (to; too; two) days for the cut to heal. _____

7. Tell the players to pick up (their; there; they're) clothes. _____

8. That store charges (to; too; two) much for soda. _____

9. I hope the campers know what (their; there; they're) doing. _____

10. (Their; There; They're) are more copies of the book on the shelf. _____

11. Take this book (to; too; two) the library. _____

12. (Their; There; They're) going to take the train to El Paso. _____

13. I can only stay for (to; too; two) minutes. _____

14. All workers should know (their; there; they're) duties. _____

Ⓓ Proofread and Write

Julio took the following notes as he read his history book. He made three spelling mistakes. Cross out the misspelled words. Write the correct spellings above them.

> In wartime, many African Americans have answered there country's call.
>
> In the Civil War, black soldiers served with pride and devotion. Many did not survive the war.
>
> In Werld War II, they flew fighter planes in one battle after another.
>
> In Vietnam and in the Gulf War, black soldiers bravely took the feild against the enemy.

Reread the paragraph on page 92. Take some notes on what you read. Use at least three list words.

_____

_____

_____

_____

_____

Writing Portfolio

Proofread your notes carefully. Correct any mistakes. Then make a clean copy and put it in your writing portfolio.

20 A Changing Job

Ⓐ Check the Meaning

Read the paragraph below. Think about the meaning of the words in bold type.

The job of the **military** has changed with time. In the past, a nation used its army and navy to **destroy** an enemy. The **foe** was often a nation that attacked a **loyal** neighbor. Victory was the result of a **strong** fighting force. This is not always the way it is today. Now the military is used for other kinds of **trouble**. An army may become the **police** in a country that needs law and order. It may stop the fighting between two warring groups. A navy may help to save people at sea. These people may be trying to **escape** an unjust place. The military services often work **together**. They may try to keep the **peace** while people vote. The jobs have changed, but the work is still dangerous.

Write each word in bold type next to its meaning. Check your answers in the Mini-Dictionary.

_____ **1.** freedom from war or disagreements

_____ **2.** with another person, group, or thing

_____ **3.** an enemy

_____ **4.** the army, navy, or air force

_____ **5.** having power or strength

_____ **6.** faithful

_____ **7.** difficulty or danger

_____ **8.** people who make sure laws are obeyed

_____ **9.** to wreck or ruin

_____ **10.** to get free of

Score: ⟋ 10

B Study the Spelling

Word List

trouble	foe	peace	military	destroy
strong	police	escape	loyal	together

Change the underlined letter or letters. Write a list word.

1. stri<u>ng</u> _____

2. <u>t</u>oe _____

3. <u>r</u>oyal _____

4. poli<u>t</u>e _____

5. p<u>l</u>ace _____

6. es<u>ta</u>te _____

Write the list word or words for each clue.

7. It begins with three consonants. _____

8. It rhymes with *double*. _____

9. They have the vowel sound you hear in *toy*.

   _____ _____

10. They begins and end with the same letter.

    _____ _____

11. They have just one syllable.

    _____ _____ _____

12. This word comes first in alphabetical order. _____

Write the list words with three or more syllables. Use dots between the syllables.

13. _____

14. _____

Add the missing letters. Write the list word.

15. tr___ub___e _____

16. mil___t___ry _____

17. p___l___ce _____

18. tog___th___r _____

Ⓒ Build Your Skills

Language Tutor

Nouns name persons, places, or things. A proper noun names a particular person, place, or thing. A proper noun always begins with a capital letter.

	Common Noun	**Proper Noun**
A group:	the military	the U.S. Navy
Someone:	a man	Joe Louis
A place:	a city	Mexico City
A thing:	a lake	Lake Superior

Write these sentences. Begin each proper noun with a capital letter.

1. The union army was led by ulysses s. grant.

_____

2. A treaty was signed in paris, france.

_____

3. From our room we could see mount rushmore.

_____

4. I must take a test on the declaration of independence.

_____

5. Our shop closes on labor day.

_____

6. The trouble was reported to the dallas police department.

_____

7. Members of the hamilton garden club met last night.

_____

8. The davis street bridge was closed yesterday.

_____

Score: ⟋ 8

Ⓓ Proofread and Write

Katrina wrote some questions she wanted to ask her history teacher. She made three spelling
mistakes. She also forget to begin a proper noun with a capital letter. Cross out the misspelled words.
Write the correct spellings above them. Also write the capital letter above where it should be.

- Where are the trouble spots in the
  world today?

- Which countries are the strong
  militery powers?

- Was a peice treaty signed at the end
  of the korean War?

- How many Jews were able to excape
  Germany?

- Did any southern states stay loyal to
  the United States?

Make a list of questions you would like to ask one of your teachers. Use at least three list words.

_____

_____

_____

_____

_____

Writing Portfolio

Proofread your list carefully. Correct any mistakes. Then make a clean copy to
take to class or put in your writing portfolio.

Unit 5 Review

Finish the Meaning

Fill in the circle next to the word that best completes each sentence.

1. The _____ includes the army, the air force, and the navy.

   Ⓐ cafeteria   Ⓒ laundry
   Ⓑ police   Ⓓ military

2. She worked long hours. She had great _____ to her job.

   Ⓐ answer   Ⓒ labor
   Ⓑ devotion   Ⓓ business

3. Jerry fought back. He had a right to _____ himself.

   Ⓐ vote   Ⓒ defend
   Ⓑ achieve   Ⓓ contain

4. We won 77 to 42. It was an easy _____.

   Ⓐ victory   Ⓒ doubt
   Ⓑ fine   Ⓓ package

5. Do not fall into the ocean. A person cannot _____ long in freezing water.

   Ⓐ bathe   Ⓒ receive
   Ⓑ survive   Ⓓ clean

6. I have known her for twenty years. She is a(n) _____ friend.

   Ⓐ brief   Ⓒ early
   Ⓑ final   Ⓓ loyal

7. Be friendly. _____ conduct only loses friends.

   Ⓐ Strong   Ⓒ Sweet
   Ⓑ Hostile   Ⓓ Careless

8. In war, fear can be a soldier's biggest _____.

   Ⓐ foe   Ⓒ neighbor
   Ⓑ judge   Ⓓ business

9. We went to hear a _____ by a well-known writer last night.

   Ⓐ truth   Ⓒ speech
   Ⓑ library   Ⓓ letter

10. Stealing is a _____.

    Ⓐ guess   Ⓒ lease
    Ⓑ reward   Ⓓ crime

11. The woman could _____ that she was not the cause of the accident.

    Ⓐ prove   Ⓒ care
    Ⓑ lose   Ⓓ delay

12. The senator will _____ his desire to be re-elected.

    Ⓐ achieve   Ⓒ recover
    Ⓑ allow   Ⓓ declare

GO ON ▶

Check the Spelling

Fill in the circle next to the word that is spelled correctly and best completes each sentence.

13. Sunlight can _____ the film.

  Ⓐ distroy   Ⓒ destrouy

  Ⓑ destroy   Ⓓ dastroy

14. The tree fell and made an _____ noise.

  Ⓐ awfull   Ⓒ aweful

  Ⓑ afful   Ⓓ awful

15. Which _____ has the best record?

  Ⓐ partie   Ⓒ party

  Ⓑ pardy   Ⓓ parety

16. The workers took _____ break at noon.

  Ⓐ their   Ⓒ thir

  Ⓑ thier   Ⓓ thur

17. The county hopes to build a new _____ next year.

  Ⓐ jayle   Ⓒ jale

  Ⓑ jial   Ⓓ jail

18. The teacher had a _____ that all students could do well.

  Ⓐ belief   Ⓒ balief

  Ⓑ beleaf   Ⓓ beleif

19. The_____ raged for days.

  Ⓐ batle   Ⓒ battle

  Ⓑ battel   Ⓓ baddle

20. Sam likes the _____ and quiet of the early morning.

  Ⓐ piece   Ⓒ peece

  Ⓑ peace   Ⓓ paece

21. There will be a lot of _____ on the bridge this weekend.

  Ⓐ trafic   Ⓒ traffick

  Ⓑ traffic   Ⓓ traffik

22. Our dog runs through the _____ near our house.

  Ⓐ field   Ⓒ feald

  Ⓑ feeld   Ⓓ feild

23. We hope to _____ from the city this weekend.

  Ⓐ excape   Ⓒ escape

  Ⓑ eskape   Ⓓ escaip

24. They made a _____ search for the lost child.

  Ⓐ through   Ⓒ thorow

  Ⓑ therough   Ⓓ thorough

STOP

Score: /24

Getting Things Done

Ⓐ Check the Meaning

Read the paragraph below. Think about the meaning of the words in bold type.

There are many things that can create a **demand** on one's time. For example, taking a child to a soccer game or making a **date** to have lunch with a friend. We hardly **finish** one thing when something else must be done. Will you be **able** to **remember** it all? If you make a plan, you will not **forget** to do important things. At the **beginning** of the week, make seven lists of things to do. Make one list for each day of the week. Write the day at the top of the page. **Below** it, have people in your home list what they need to do that day. You may have to **limit** the number of things each person can list. If you have one car, you may not be **able** to do everything. As a **group**, figure out what is most important. Go over this list with everyone each morning.

Write each word in bold type next to its meaning. Check your answers in the Mini-Dictionary.

_____ **1.** under; in a lower place

_____ **2.** the first part; the place where something starts

_____ **3.** a very strong request or need

_____ **4.** having the skills needed to do something

_____ **5.** the day when something is to happen

_____ **6.** a number of people or things together

_____ **7.** to bring back to mind

_____ **8.** to keep within a certain number or border

_____ **9.** to bring to the end; to complete

_____ **10.** to fail to think about

B Study the Spelling

Word List

limit	group	below	forget	date
remember	able	demand	finish	beginning

Form a list word by matching the beginning of a word in the first column with its ending in the second column. Write the list word.

a   it   **1.** _____

de   low   **2.** _____

fin   ble   **3.** _____

lim   ish   **4.** _____

be   mand   **5.** _____

Write the list word or words for each clue.

6. They have three syllables. _____ _____

7. It ends with a vowel, consonant, and *e*. _____

8. It begins with two consonants. _____

9. They end with two consonants. _____

_____ _____

10. It is formed from the word *begin*. _____

11. The word *member* is part of its spelling. _____

12. The word *get* is part of its spelling. _____

13. It rhymes with *late*. _____

14. It begins like *because* and ends like *shallow*. _____

Circle the list word in these longer words. Then write the list word.

15. unable _____   **18.** forgetful _____

16. regroup _____   **19.** unlimited _____

17. refinish _____   **20.** demanding _____

C Build Your Skills

Language Tutor

Business letters have six parts: the heading, the inside address, the greeting, the body, the closing, and the signature. Study the example on the next page.

Five parts are missing from the letter below. Add the five parts. The letter is for Ms. Joan Kirkwood, the owner of The Book Trader. Her shop is at 454 West Avenue, Belleville, IL 60023. Use your own name and address.

① _____
_____
_____

② _____
_____
_____
_____

③ _____

I have not been able to find a copy of *Baseball is a Funny Game*. I think the book was written by Joe Garagiola. If you have a copy, I would like to buy it. Please let me know if you have the book and what the price would be.

④ _____

⑤ _____

Ⓓ Proofread and Write

Ms. Lake wrote this letter to her son's soccer coach. She was careful to use all six parts of a business letter, but she made three spelling mistakes. Cross out the misspelled words. Write the correct spellings above them.

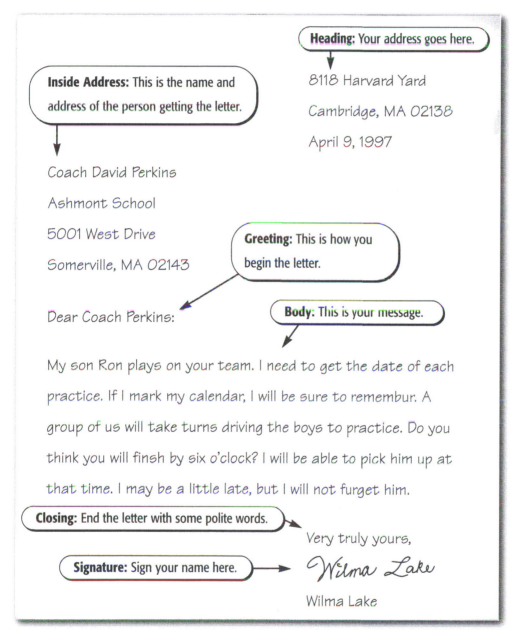

Heading: Your address goes here.

8118 Harvard Yard

Cambridge, MA 02138

April 9, 1997

Inside Address: This is the name and address of the person getting the letter.

Coach David Perkins

Ashmont School

5001 West Drive

Somerville, MA 02143

Greeting: This is how you begin the letter.

Dear Coach Perkins:

Body: This is your message.

My son Ron plays on your team. I need to get the date of each practice. If I mark my calendar, I will be sure to remembur. A group of us will take turns driving the boys to practice. Do you think you will finsh by six o'clock? I will be able to pick him up at that time. I may be a little late, but I will not furget him.

Closing: End the letter with some polite words.

Very truly yours,

Signature: Sign your name here.

Wilma Lake

Wilma Lake

Writing Portfolio

Write a letter of your own. Use your own paper. Ask for facts or news about an event. Include all six parts of a business letter. Use at least three list words.

Proofread your letter carefully and correct any mistakes. Then make a clean copy to mail or put in your writing portfolio.

22 Planning a Report

Ⓐ Check the Meaning

Read the paragraph below. Think about the meaning of the words in bold type.

Writing a report is not easy. Some people have the **idea** that you just start writing **about** whatever comes to mind. It's not that **simple**. A report done this way will just **confuse** the reader. A lot of work must be done before you begin to write. First **decide** on the **purpose** of the report. It helps to write the purpose in a **notebook** or on a piece of paper. Then try to **recall** things that will help you achieve your purpose. If you are not sure about something, list it anyway. Next, look over your list. Cross out anything that doesn't make **sense** to include. Put what is left into groups that go together. Begin the report by telling your purpose. Then take up each group one at a time. Doing a report this way gives you a better **chance** of being understood.

Write each word in bold type next to its meaning. Check your answers in the Mini-Dictionary.

_____	**1.** to call back; to bring back to the memory
_____	**2.** good judgment
_____	**3.** having to do with
_____	**4.** easy; not difficult
_____	**5.** to mix up or to puzzle
_____	**6.** possibility; likelihood
_____	**7.** a book with pages to write on
_____	**8.** a belief or thought in the mind
_____	**9.** the desired goal or aim
_____	**10.** to make up one's mind

Score: ⟋ 10

B Study the Spelling

Word List

sim<u>ple</u>	<u>note</u>book	sense	about	purpose
idea	chance	confuse	decide	recall

Replace the underlined letters to write a list word.

1. si<u>nc</u>e _____

2. re<u>fi</u>ll _____

3. s<u>a</u>mple _____

4. abo<u>ve</u> _____

5. con<u>cer</u>n _____

6. de<u>fen</u>d _____

7. <u>cook</u>book _____

8. <u>gl</u>ance _____

Write the list word or words for each clue.

9. It ends with a double consonant. _____

10. They end with *se*. _____

_____ _____

11. It has four letters and three syllables. _____

12. It has six letters and one syllable. _____

13. It is made from two words and has a double vowel. _____

14. It begins with a prefix that means "again." _____

15. It rhymes with *fence*. _____

16. It begins like *aboard* and ends like *shout*. _____

Write *purpose*, *simple*, *idea*, and *decide* in alphabetical order. Use dots between the syllables.

17. _____   19. _____

18. _____   20. _____

C Build Your Skills

Language Tutor

Sometimes a word at the end of a line must be broken. Always break a work between syllables. Check a dictionary if you are not sure of the syllables. Use a hyphen or short dash to show that the word has been broken.

Don't miss the meeting tomorrow. The purpose of the meeting is to elect officers.

Use a hyphen in all compound numbers from twenty-one to ninety-nine.

twenty-two   forty-seven   eighty-six   ninety-three

Suppose each word came at the end of a line. Write each word. Add the hyphen where it belongs.

1. simple _____

2. decide _____

3. parent _____

4. seldom _____

5. machine _____

6. stomach _____

7. because _____

8. notebook _____

Write these sentences. Break the sentence within the underlined word. Add hyphens where needed.

9. Twenty six people will be at the <u>meeting</u>. They will want answers to their questions.

_____

_____

10. I need help with my <u>homework</u>. I do not know how to do number thirty one.

_____

_____

11. Jerry never travels by plane. There must be a <u>reason</u> why he dislikes planes.

_____

_____

12. My notes from chapter thirty two are in my <u>notebook</u>. I will get them after class.

_____

_____

D Proofread and Write

Belinda wrote these notes for a report on her dog, Bailey. She made three spelling mistakes. Cross out the misspelled words. Write the correct spellings above them.

Purpose: To tell abowt my dog, Bailey

Bailey has good sence. She knows when it is time

to eat. The phone and doorbell do not confuse her.

She goes to the one that is ringing.

Bailey loves her ball. She is able to recal where she

left it. She follows simple commands. She knows to

go to her bed. She also knows not to chase cars.

I feed her when she barks. I cannot decide if I

trained Bailey or if Bailey trained me.

Write some notes you might use in a report. It can be about a family member or any other topic. Use at least three list words.

_____

_____

_____

_____

Writing Portfolio

Proofread your notes carefully. Correct any mistakes. Then make a clean copy and put it in your writing portfolio.

23 Remembering What You Read

Ⓐ Check the Meaning

Read the paragraph below. Think about the meaning of the words in bold type.

Have you ever read for an **hour** only to find you were not **sure** what you had read? If so, you are not **alone**. Many readers make the mistake of trying to remember every small **detail**. This usually cannot be done. Rather than trying to remember every **fact**, try to **understand** what the facts mean. You may not recall how much fat and other things are in a hot dog or an apple. You can remember which one is better for you. As you read, make an **outline**. The **proper** way to do this is to stop from time to time. Write down the main idea in what you have just read. Under it, list the important facts that back up this idea. You can **return** to this outline later to **review** what you have read.

Write each word in bold type next to its meaning. Check your answers in the Mini-Dictionary.

_____ **1.** correct; suitable for a purpose

_____ **2.** a smaller or less important item

_____ **3.** a point-by-point summary of information

_____ **4.** certain; without doubt

_____ **5.** an amount of time equal to sixty minutes

_____ **6.** to go back to

_____ **7.** to get the meaning of; to know

_____ **8.** something known to be true

_____ **9.** by oneself; with no other person

_____ **10.** to go over again; to study

B Study the Spelling

Word List

proper	return	detail	fact	sure
hour	alone	understand	review	outline

Write the list word or words for each clue.

1. The word *turn* is part of its spelling. _____

2. They are made from two smaller words.

   _____ _____

3. They begin with the *re-* prefix. _____ _____

4. It rhymes with *power.* _____

5. It has three syllables. _____

6. It rhymes with *cure.* _____

7. It has two syllables. The first syllable has just one letter. _____

8. The word *tail* is part of its spelling. _____

9. It has one syllable. It ends with two consonants. _____

10. It begins with two consonants. _____

Add the missing syllable. Write the list word.

11. _____tail _____

12. a_____ _____

13. _____turn _____

14. _____line _____

15. prop_____ _____

One word in each group is misspelled. Circle the misspelled word. Write it correctly.

16. understand   shure   return   _____

17. reveiw   outline   alone   _____

18. detail   proper   howr   _____

Ⓒ Build Your Skills

Language Tutor

A suffix is a word part added to the end of a word. The *-ly* suffix changes how the word is used.

You must have the <u>proper</u> tools for the job.

The tools must be used <u>properly</u>.

If the word ends with *y*, change *y* to *i* before adding *-ly*.

Enid seems very <u>happy</u>. She is singing <u>happily</u>.

Write these sentences. Add *-ly* to the underlined word to find the missing word.

1. Please be <u>careful</u> on the job. Read the safety rules _____.

_____

2. You must be <u>quiet</u>. Walk through the room _____.

_____

3. Everyone seemed very <u>sad</u>. They spoke _____ of the loss.

_____

4. The dog was <u>hungry</u>. It _____ gulped down the food.

_____

5. It was a <u>slow</u> ride into town. The cars _____ crawled down the highway.

_____

6. What a <u>lazy</u> cat! It _____ sleeps in the sun all day.

_____

7. The player became <u>angry</u>. He _____ slammed his hat to the ground.

_____

8. We need a <u>quick</u> meal. What can be made _____?

_____

D Proofread and Write

Ken made a list of good study habits he wants to use. He made three spelling mistakes. Cross out the misspelled words. Write the correct spellings above them.

1. Always bring home the proper books.

2. Set aside at least one our to review the homework.

3. Try to do the work aloan. If I do not understand something, ask for help.

4. List the main ideas in each chapter. Under each main idea, write any detail that goes with it.

5. Use this owtline to study for the test.

6. Be sure to answer all the questions at the end of the chapter.

Make a list of things you do to help yourself study. Use at least three list words.

_____

_____

_____

Writing Portfolio

Proofread your list carefully. Correct any mistakes. Then make a clean copy and put it in your writing portfolio.

24 Moving On

(A) Check the Meaning

Read the paragraph below. Think about the meaning of the words in bold type.

Everyone has the **power** to bring about **change**. Change can be good or bad. It depends on the person and the change. From time to time many people feel the need to change jobs. Such an important change should not be made for **foolish** reasons. It needs careful **thought**. One bad day is no reason to quit. Yet there is no **reason** to be **afraid** of change either, if it is done right. Do you have a **skill** that is not being used in your job? What kind of job would make good use of that skill? Do not **overlook** some **talent** that you could work to make better. Someone who enjoys cooking might go to school to become a baker. Such change may not come about easily. It happens only to those who **refuse** to just stay put.

Write each word in bold type next to its meaning. Check your answers in the Mini-Dictionary.

_____ **1.** full of fear

_____ **2.** the ability or strength to do something very well

_____ **3.** to be unwilling to do something

_____ **4.** unwise; without good sense

_____ **5.** to fail to see or notice

_____ **6.** an ability someone is born with

_____ **7.** the strength or ability to do something

_____ **8.** to make different

_____ **9.** the act of thinking; careful attention

_____ **10.** the cause for an action

Score: /10

B Study the Spelling

Word List				
skill	refuse	thought	power	afraid
talent	overlook	foolish	reason	change

Write the list word for each clue.

1. It ends with a double consonant. _____

2. It is made from two smaller words. _____

3. It has seven letters but just one syllable. _____

4. It comes from the word *fool*. _____

5. It has a silent *gh* in its spelling. _____

6. It begins like *sky* and ends like *will*. _____

7. It has only one syllable. It rhymes with *strange*. _____

8. The word *raid* is part of its spelling. _____

Write *talent*, *reason*, *power*, and *refuse* in alphabetical order. Use dots between the syllables.

9. _____   11. _____

10. _____   12. _____

Add the missing letters. Write the words.

13. po____ ___r _____

14. r___fu___e _____

15. tal____ ___t _____

16. re____s___n _____

17. ov___rlo___k _____

18. ch___ng___ _____

19. ___o___lis___ _____

20. af___ai___ _____

Score: /20

C Build Your Skills

Language Tutor

A dictionary tells you how to say a word. It does this by respelling the word with special letters. These special letters always stand for the same sounds.

Word	Dictionary Spelling
thought	thôt
change	chānj
talent	**tăl′** ənt
care	kâr
foolish	**fōō′** lĭsh
power	**pou′** ər

Study the list of sounds and their special letters on page 122.

Study these sound spellings. Write the word that matches the sound spelling.

1. skĭl	skin	school	skill	_____
2. shōŏr	sure	sour	cure	_____
3. făkt	fake	flat	fact	_____
4. kwĭk	kick	quick	cent	_____
5. strông	song	sting	strong	_____
6. rĕd′ ē	ready	red	really	_____
7. fôr **gĕt′**	forty	forget	four	_____
8. ə **bŭv′**	about	around	above	_____
9. ûrn	earn	under	early	_____
10. brôt	brag	brought	bat	_____
11. chîr	cheer	chair	chapter	_____
12. ôl′ mōst′	always	almost	older	_____
13. mĭ **stāk′**	misspell	missing	mistake	_____
14. jŭj	judge	jug	jump	_____
15. ô′ fəl	offer	awful	answer	_____

Score: ___ / 15

Ⓓ Proofread and Write

Ann was looking for a job. She made a list of her good qualities that would interest an employer. She made three spelling mistakes. Cross out the misspelled words. Write the correct spellings above them.

My Good Qualities

- I have a talent for working with others.

- I am not afrade to work long hours.

- I never overlook small details.

- I have the skill to use all kinds of power tools.

- I rafuse to do anything less than my best work.

- My last boss thought I was her best worker.

- I never give some foolish reeson for coming to work late.

Writing Portfolio

Make a list of your best qualities. Use your own paper. Include everything that would interest an employer. Use at least three list words.

Proofread your list carefully. Correct any mistakes. Then make a clean copy and put it in your writing portfolio.

Unit 6 Review

Finish the Meaning

Fill in the circle next to the word that best completes each sentence.

1. The book is hard to follow. Few people _____ it right away.

   (A) require   (C) answer
   (B) understand   (D) deliver

2. A good writer tries not to _____ the reader.

   (A) confuse   (C) recall
   (B) achieve   (D) wrinkle

3. Remember to buy everything on the shopping list. Do not _____ anything.

   (A) destroy   (C) support
   (B) chance   (D) overlook

4. Serving on the school board was a big _____ on Ann's time. It was a lot of work.

   (A) escape   (C) crime
   (B) demand   (D) chance

5. You must have a good _____ to miss work.

   (A) reason   (C) habit
   (B) skill   (D) reward

6. Those stores _____ the number of sale items you may buy.

   (A) declare   (C) earn
   (B) rescue   (D) limit

7. A waiter should know the _____ way to set a table.

   (A) foolish   (C) careless
   (B) proper   (D) final

8. Write down the phone number. We will need to _____ it later.

   (A) recall   (C) recover
   (B) forget   (D) apply

9. Sam wrote down the main ideas. He used this _____ to study.

   (A) window   (C) outline
   (B) fact   (D) lease

10. It is cold in the winter. It makes _____ to wear a warm coat.

    (A) labor   (C) peace
    (B) sense   (D) trouble

11. We should make a list. We can never _____ everything.

    (A) finish   (C) handle
    (B) declare   (D) remember

12. I could not _____ such a kind offer.

    (A) refuse   (C) survive
    (B) support   (D) vote

GO ON ➤

Check the Spelling

Fill in the circle next to the word that is spelled correctly and best completes each sentence.

13. Ben _____ the game was over.

   Ⓐ thaught   Ⓒ thought
   Ⓑ thout   Ⓓ thouoght

14. Today we will see a film _____ fire safety.

   Ⓐ abowt   Ⓒ abaut
   Ⓑ abuot   Ⓓ about

15. Always _____ what you have read before a big test.

   Ⓐ review   Ⓒ raview
   Ⓑ revew   Ⓓ reveiw

16. Fran should be _____ to run the race next week.

   Ⓐ abel   Ⓒ able
   Ⓑ abbel   Ⓓ abell

17. You could see her _____ for art by looking at the painting.

   Ⓐ talunt   Ⓒ tallent
   Ⓑ talent   Ⓓ talint

18. No _____ was given for the meeting.

   Ⓐ perpose   Ⓒ purpos
   Ⓑ purpoise   Ⓓ purpose

19. Many children are _____ of the dark.

   Ⓐ afraid   Ⓒ affraid
   Ⓑ afrade   Ⓓ afreid

20. Do not miss the _____ of the movie.

   Ⓐ begining   Ⓒ begenning
   Ⓑ baginning   Ⓓ beginning

21. It took Jim an _____ to read the paper.

   Ⓐ our   Ⓒ hour
   Ⓑ howr   Ⓓ huor

22. There were four girls in each _____.

   Ⓐ group   Ⓒ gruop
   Ⓑ groop   Ⓓ grupe

23. We did the job well. We did not forget a single _____.

   Ⓐ ditail   Ⓒ detale
   Ⓑ detayl   Ⓓ detail

24. The waiter is coming. We must _____ what to order.

   Ⓐ dacide   Ⓒ decide
   Ⓑ deside   Ⓓ daside

STOP

Score: ___ / 24

Post-test

Part 1: Meaning

For each item below, fill in the letter next to the word or phrase that most nearly expresses the meaning of the first word.

> **Sample**
>
> hammer
> - (A) part of the arm
> - ● a tool used for driving nails
> - (C) a type of vegetable
> - (D) to mix thoroughly

1. require
   - (A) to ask about again
   - (B) to need
   - (C) to sing in a group
   - (D) to get or gain

2. habit
   - (A) a dark covering
   - (B) a pipe for carrying water
   - (C) a place to live
   - (D) an action done over and over

3. employer
   - (A) someone who pays people to work
   - (B) a trick
   - (C) someone who works for money
   - (D) a ruler

4. course
   - (A) a rough cloth
   - (B) an unusual food
   - (C) a class in school
   - (D) an open space

5. declare
   - (A) a sweet dessert
   - (B) to state in a strong way
   - (C) to give up
   - (D) to fix

6. thorough
   - (A) complete
   - (B) finished
   - (C) between
   - (D) pure

7. refuse
   - (A) to give up
   - (B) to make smaller
   - (C) to be unwilling to do something
   - (D) to use up

8. detail
   - (A) something less important
   - (B) a strong dislike
   - (C) a change in direction
   - (D) a thought or idea

9. daily
   - (A) to slow down
   - (B) to act without thinking of others
   - (C) having a soiled or worn-out look
   - (D) happening every day

10. category
    - (A) a book listing things for sale
    - (B) a group of things
    - (C) a deep ditch or valley
    - (D) an animal in the cat family

GO ON ►

Part 2: Spelling

For each item below, fill in the letter next to the correct spelling of the word.

11. (A) nieghbor   (C) neighbor
    (B) neighber   (D) neigber

12. (A) coller   (C) coler
    (B) collar   (D) collur

13. (A) tragedy   (C) tradagy
    (B) tragday   (D) tragidy

14. (A) sence   (C) scense
    (B) sense   (D) scence

15. (A) traffac   (C) trafic
    (B) traffick   (D) traffic

16. (A) milatary   (C) military
    (B) milatery   (D) millatary

17. (A) doubt   (C) dowbt
    (B) dout   (D) doute

18. (A) allthough   (C) althou
    (B) although   (D) althow

19. (A) abcent   (C) abscent
    (B) absent   (D) absunt

20. (A) peril   (C) peral
    (B) pearil   (D) perile

21. (A) kwart   (C) quort
    (B) quart   (D) kwert

22. (A) baught   (C) bowt
    (B) bot   (D) bought

23. (A) trousers   (C) trouzers
    (B) trowsers   (D) trowzers

24. (A) misteak   (C) mistake
    (B) masteak   (D) misstake

25. (A) bellow   (C) beloe
    (B) balow   (D) below

26. (A) stile   (C) styel
    (B) stiel   (D) style

27. (A) danger   (C) dangur
    (B) danjer   (D) dainger

28. (A) peeple   (C) peaple
    (B) people   (D) peopel

29. (A) afrayd   (C) afraid
    (B) afrade   (D) ufraid

30. (A) labur   (C) laybor
    (B) laibor   (D) labor

STOP

Score: ___/30

How to Use the Dictionary

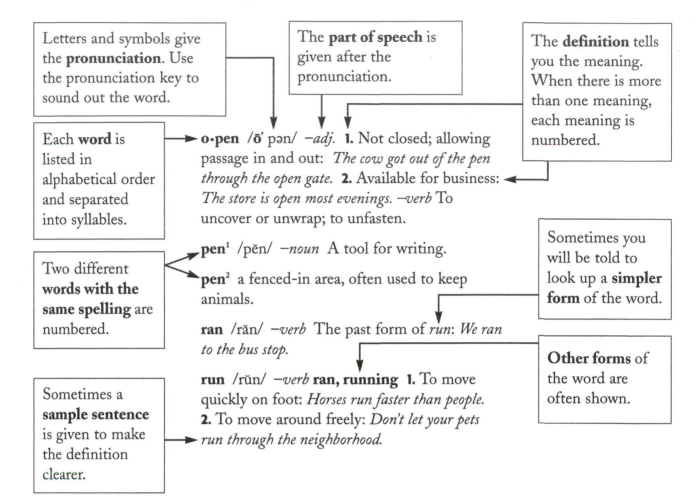

Letters and symbols give the **pronunciation**. Use the pronunciation key to sound out the word.

The **part of speech** is given after the pronunciation.

The **definition** tells you the meaning. When there is more than one meaning, each meaning is numbered.

Each **word** is listed in alphabetical order and separated into syllables.

o·pen /ō′ pən/ —*adj*. **1.** Not closed; allowing passage in and out: *The cow got out of the pen through the open gate.* **2.** Available for business: *The store is open most evenings.* —*verb* To uncover or unwrap; to unfasten.

pen¹ /pĕn/ —*noun* A tool for writing.

pen² a fenced-in area, often used to keep animals.

Two different **words with the same spelling** are numbered.

Sometimes you will be told to look up a **simpler form** of the word.

ran /răn/ —*verb* The past form of *run*: *We ran to the bus stop.*

Other forms of the word are often shown.

run /rŭn/ —*verb* **ran, running 1.** To move quickly on foot: *Horses run faster than people.* **2.** To move around freely: *Don't let your pets run through the neighborhood.*

Sometimes a **sample sentence** is given to make the definition clearer.

Pronunciation Key

ă	cat	ī	ice	o͞o	food	hw	which
ā	day	î	near	yo͞o	cute	zh	usual
â	care	ŏ	hot	o͝o	book	ə	about
ä	father	ō	go	ŭ	drum		open
ĕ	wet	ô	law	û	fur		pencil
ē	see	oi	oil	*th*	this		lemon
ĭ	pit	ou	out	th	thin		circus

Mini-Dictionary

a·ble /ā′ bəl/ -*adj.* Having what is needed to do something: *Do you think he is able to do this job?*

a·bout /ə bout′/ -*preposition* Concerning; having to do with: *I read a book about computers last week.*

a·bove /ə bŭv′/ -*adverb* At a higher level; overhead: *The ceiling above our heads is cracked.*

ab·sent /ăb′ sənt/ -*adj.* Not present; not where one should be: *Please do not be absent from work on Friday, because we need all our workers to help with this order.*

a·chieve /ə chēv′/ -*verb* **achieved, achieving, achieves** To meet a goal or accomplish something: *To achieve your goals, you must have a plan.*

ac·tive /ăk′ tĭv/ -*adj.* Moving about; lively: *Active children do not sit still for very long.*

a·fraid /ə frād′/ -*adj.* Full of fear: *Small children are sometimes afraid of large dogs.*

a·gree /ə grē′/ -*verb* **agreed, agreeing, agrees** 1. To have the same opinion; to see things the same way: *We all agree the movie is great.* 2. To say one is willing; to commit to something: *Will you agree to clean the bathroom this week?*

al·low /ə lou′/ -*verb* To let happen; to permit: *Will you allow me to take a break at ten o'clock?*

al·most /ôl′ mōst′/ -*adverb* Very close to; nearly: *I am almost finished with the cleaning; I have only one room left.*

a·lone /ə lōn′/ -*adj.* By oneself; without any other person or thing: *With her family out of town, Doretha spent a quiet day alone.*

al·read·y /ôl rĕd′ ē/ -*adverb* By this time, before: *When we reached the station, the bus was already there.*

al·though /ôl *th*ō′/ -*conjunction* Even though; despite: *Although you are not done, you will have to stop working now.*

al·ways /ôl′ wāz/ -*adverb* At all times: *I never forget my keys; I always bring them with me.*

a·mong /ə mŭng′/ -*preposition* In the middle of: *I found this recipe among my old cookbooks.*

an·oth·er /ə nŭ*th*′ ər/ -*adj.* 1. Being one more; additional. 2. Being different: *We will visit Aunt Sue another day.*

an·swer /ăn′ sər/ -*noun* 1. A response or reply to something such as an offer, question, letter, or request: *I mailed my answer to your letter last week.* 2. A way to solve a problem. -*verb* To respond or reply.

ap·ply /ə plī′/ -*verb* **applied, applying, applies** 1. To ask for: *We will apply for a loan to buy a house.* 2. To put on: *Apply two coats of paint to this chair.*

ar·rive /ə rīv′/ -*verb* **arrived, arriving, arrives** To get to a place: *We will arrive in Boston by noon.*

as·sist /ə sĭst′/ -*verb* (To help:) *Find someone to assist you with that heavy load.*

aw·ful /ô′ fəl/ -*adj.* Very bad or unpleasant; horrible: *The play was awful because it had no plot.*

back /băk/ -*noun* The part of the body opposite the chest that reaches from the neck to the hips.

ba·nan·a /bə năn′ ə/ -*noun* A long, curved fruit with a yellow or reddish skin and soft flesh.

bathe /bāth/ -verb **bathed, bathing, bathes**
To wash oneself or something else: *Sid always bathes after working in the barn.*

bat·tle /băt´l/ -noun **1.** A fight between two groups, usually with weapons. **2.** A hard struggle or contest.

beach /bēch/ -noun The sandy or rocky area where land meets water: *Bring swimsuits and shovels when you go to the beach.*

be·cause /bĭ kôz´/ -conjunction For that reason: *I cannot run today because I broke by foot.*

be·gin·ning /bĭ gĭn´ĭng/ -noun **1.** The first part. **2.** The time or place where something starts.

be·lief /bĭ lēf´/ -noun An idea held to be true, especially about something that is difficult to prove: *Todd's belief in the power of positive thinking helped him win the race.*

be·low /bĭ lō´/ -adverb Under; in a lower place: *We found a tunnel below the old mansion.*

bi·cy·cle /bī´ sĭk´ əl/ -noun A two-wheeled vehicle with a seat and handlebars powered by pushing on the pedals: *Sandy rides her bicycle to work when it is not raining.*

bod·y /bŏd´ ē/ -noun The whole physical part of a person or animal: *Ted tried to squeeze his body through a hole in the fence.*

book /bo͝ok/ -noun Pages fastened together and placed between covers: *Sam liked the book so much, he couldn't put it down.*

bought /bôt/ -verb Past tense and past participle of *buy*: *I bought a new lamp for the bedroom.*

bounce /bouns/ -verb **bounced, bouncing, bounces** To spring back or jump: *This rubber ball will bounce at least three feet into the air.*

bridge /brĭj/ -noun A structure built over water or roads so people, cars, or trains can cross over.

brief /brēf/ -adj. Short in length or lasting a short time: *We will have a brief meeting before the show.*

bring /brĭng/ -verb **brought, bringing, brings** To take or carry: *Bring a pencil to every class.*

— **brought** /brôt/ -verb Past tense and past participle of *bring*: *Everyone brought something for Kim's birthday party.*

burn /bûrn/ -noun An injury caused by fire or heat. -verb To set or be on fire.

but·ter /bŭt´ ər/ -noun A yellow fat made from cream: *Vicky always puts lots of butter and salt on her corn.*

buy /bī/ -verb **bought, buying, buys** To get an object or a service by paying for it.

caf·e·te·ri·a /kăf´ ĭ tîr´ ē ə/ -noun A place to eat where people buy food at a counter and carry it to their table, especially one in a school, hospital, or large workplace: *The cafeteria serves hot dogs and beans every Friday.*

camp /kămp/ -noun A place with tents or cabins where people live for a time or sleep overnight: *The camp in Maine has no lights or running water.*

care /kâr/ -verb **cared, caring, cares** To look after, provide for, protect: *Who will care for my plants while I am away?*

care·less /kâr´ lĭs/ -adj. Done without the necessary care or thought: *I was careless with the tools and cut my finger.*

catch /kăch/ -verb **caught, catching, catches** **1.** To seize or take hold of something that is moving. **2.** To become ill with: *Sara caught a cold from her sister.*

cat·e·go·ry /kăt′ ə gôr′ ē/ –noun A group of things that are alike in some way; *The contest had two categories: one for beginners and one for experienced cooks.*

caught /kôt/ –verb Past tense and past participle of *catch*: *I caught the paper before it flew out the window.*

cau·tious /kô′ shəs/ –adj. Careful trying to avoid danger or a mistake: *A cautious driver always wears a seat belt.*

ce·re·al /sîr′ ē əl/ –noun Seeds from wheat, rice, oats, and other grains eaten as food.

chance /chăns/ –noun The possibility or likelihood that something will happen: *The chance of falling is low if you wear a safety harness.*

change /chānj/ –verb **changed, changing, changes** To make or become different; alter: *Change your seat to get a better view.*

child /chīld/ –noun A young boy or girl: *As a child, Pat liked to play with her dolls.*

chil·dren /chĭl′ drən/ –noun Plural of *child*: *Three children played on the swings.*

choice /chois/ –noun **1.** The act of choosing between two or more things. **2.** A person or thing that one chooses: *Tom's choice for lunch is always a hamburger.*

choose /chōoz/ –verb **chose, chosen, choosing, chooses** To pick or select: *You may choose any seat you like for this class.*

cir·cle /sûr′ kəl/ –noun A ring-like line where all points are an equal distance from the center: *Draw a circle around the picture you like best.*

cit·y /sĭt′ ē/ –noun A place that is larger than a town and where many people live and work.

clean /klēn/ –verb To make free from dirt or germs: *Clean your hands with soap and water before eating.* –adj. To be free of dirt or germs.

clin·ic /klĭn′ ĭk/ –noun A place that gives medical help to people who do not need to stay overnight: *At the clinic, Cara saw a doctor who cleaned her cut and sent her home.*

clock /klŏk/ –noun An instrument that measures and shows the time of day: *The clock said 3:30, but Sue was sure it must be later.*

coin /koin/ –noun A piece of metal used as money.

col·lar /kŏl′ ər/ –noun **1.** A band of cloth around the neckline of a piece of clothing: *The collar of her dress is made of lace.* **2.** A band put around the neck of an animal.

con·fuse /kən fyōoz′/ –verb **confused, confusing, confuses** To make unclear or puzzling: *A poorly worded memo will confuse the reader.*

con·tain /kən tān′/ –verb **1.** To hold. **2.** To be made up of in whole or in part: *This drink doesn't contain any fruit juice.*

cook /kŏok/ –verb To make food ready to eat by heating it: *Cook chicken until the juices are clear.*

cost /kôst/ –noun The amount of money paid or charged for something: *The cost of milk is lower at your store.* –verb To have as a price: *Milk and bread cost $2.00 at that store.*

coun·try /kŭn′ trē/ –noun An area away from cities or towns: *We often drive in the country to see the farm animals.*

course /kôrs/ –noun **1.** A class or series of classes in school: *Jen took a course in bookkeeping and accounting at the community college.* **2.** A path.

crime /krīm/ –*noun* Something that is against the law: *Stealing is a crime.*

crumb /krŭm/ –*noun* A very small bit of food, usually bread, cake, cookie, or cracker: *When we finished eating, there wasn't a crumb of cake left.*

dai·ly /dā′ lē/ –*adj.* Done, appearing, or happening every day: *The daily mail comes just before lunchtime.*

dair·y /dâr′ ē/ –*noun* A place where milk and milk products are made or stored.

dan·ger /dān′ jər/ –*noun* Something that is likely to cause injury or harm: *Carelessness is a danger when working with machinery.*

date /dāt/ –*noun* The time when something happens or happened: *The date of the picnic is June 3.*

dead·line /dĕd′ lĭn′/ –*noun* The time when something must be finished: *The deadline for this order is next Tuesday.*

de·cide /dĭ sīd′/ –*verb* decided, deciding, decides To make up one's mind; determine: *When will you decide who gets the promotion?*

de·clare /dĭ klâr′/ –*verb* declared, declaring, declares To state or make known in a strong or formal way: *The judges will declare the contest winner tonight.*

de·fend /dĭ fĕnd′/ –*verb* **1.** To speak or act in support of. **2.** To protect.

de·lay /dĭ lā′/ –*noun* A time when something is put off or not done; a pause: *The rain caused a delay in the start of the baseball game.*

de·liv·er /dĭ lĭv′ ər/ –*verb* To take something to a person or place and leave it there: *Some stores will deliver orders to your home or office.*

de·mand /dĭ mănd′/ –*noun* A very strong need or request: *A child's demand for food increases as he or she grows older.*

de·stroy /dĭ stroi′/ –*verb* To ruin completely; make unfit for any use: *Leaving tools out in the rain can destroy them.*

de·tail /dĭ tāl′/ or /dē′ tāl′/ –*noun* A smaller part or less important part of something: *After you have the main idea, read closely for each detail.*

de·vo·tion /dĭ vō′ shən/ –*noun* Faithfulness; loyalty: *She spent many hours at work because of her devotion to her students.*

dol·lar /dŏl′ ər/ –*noun* A unit of money equal to 100 cents: *The dinner cost forty-five dollars.*

dou·ble /dŭb′ əl/ –*adj.* Twice as much as, two times: *Serena's office is through the double doors.*

doubt /dout/ –*verb* **1.** To be unsure or uncertain. **2.** To find something unlikely: *I doubt we will be able to make the deadline this week.*

ear·ly /ûr′ lē/ –*adj.* **1.** Happening before the usual or expected time: *The order was ready early, so the customer was pleased.* **2.** Happening at or near the beginning.

earn /ûrn/ –*verb* To get in return for work: *Fair bosses earn their workers' respect.*

eas·y /ē′ zē/ –*adj.* Needing little work or effort; not hard: *The test was easy; everyone passed.*

ei·ther /ē′ thər/ or /ī′ thər/ –*pronoun* One or the other: *Tim and John are coming to the party; either will help move the table.*

em·ploy·er /ĕm ploi′ ər/ –*noun* Person or business that pays others to work: *The shoe factory is the largest employer in town.*

e·nough /ĭ nŭf′/ –*adj.* As many or as much as is needed: *I have enough work to keep me busy all day.*

es·cape /ĭ skāp′/ –*verb* escaped, escaping, escapes To get free from.

e·vent /ĭ vĕnt´/ -*noun* Something that happens, especially something important or big: *The county fair is the biggest event of the summer.*

eyes /īz/ -*noun* Organs that people and animals use to see.

fact /făkt/ -*noun* Something known to be true: *It is a fact that George Washington was our first president.*

fa·mil·iar /fə mĭl´ yər/ -*adj.* Seen or heard often, well-known: *Former players are a familiar sight at the ball games.*

fam·i·ly /făm´ ə lē/ -*noun* People who live together or who share a common ancestry: *Cindy has two sisters in her family.*

field /fēld/ -*noun* An open, clear area of land.

fi·nal /fī´ nəl/ -*adj.* **1.** Last, coming at the end. **2.** Not to be changed: *The judge's decision is final.*

fine /fīn/ -*noun* Money paid as a punishment for breaking the law: *We paid a fine for parking in the wrong space.*

fin·ger /fĭng´ gər/ -*noun* One of the five parts of the human body extending from each hand: *Diana wore a lovely ring on her finger.*

fin·ish /fĭn´ ĭsh/ -*verb* To complete; to bring or come to an end.

flour /flour/ -*noun* A powder made from a grain such as wheat, or from beans, or potatoes: *It takes four cups of flour to make this cake.*

foe /fō/ -*noun* An enemy.

fool·ish /foo´ lĭsh/ -*adj.* Unwise; without good sense; silly.

for·get /fər gĕt´/ -*verb* **forgot, forgotten, forgetting, forgets** To fail to remember or bring to mind: *Write things down if you often forget what you need to do.*

fruit /froot/ -*noun* The part of a plant that holds seeds and that may be eaten: *Apples, peaches, grapes, and pears are my favorite fruits.*

gog·gles /gŏg´ əlz/ -*noun* Glasses worn to protect the eyes: *When the glass shattered close to his face, Tim was glad he was wearing his goggles.*

grain /grān/ -*noun* The seeds of wheat, corn, rice, and other plants that may be eaten.

group /groop/ -*noun* A number of persons or things being, belonging, or acting together: *A group of employees went to the boss to ask for better training.*

guess /gĕs/ -*verb* To decide without enough information to be sure: *I've never been there, but I guess the trip will take two hours.*

hab·it /hăb´ ĭt/ -*noun* An activity or action done so often that it takes no thinking or planning to do: *Beth takes the bus to work out of habit.*

half /hăf/ -*noun* One of two equal parts.

hand·book /hănd´ book´/ -*noun* A book of information or facts: *We have a handbook that tells about the workers' health plan.*

han·dle /hăn´ dl/ -*noun* The part of a tool or door that is made to be held: *The handle of the coffeepot was too hot to touch.*

height /hīt/ -*noun* The length from bottom to top: *The height of the wall is six feet.*

high·way /hī´ wā´/ -*noun* A large, paved, public road: *Take the highway if you want the fastest route.*

home·work /hōm´ wûrk´/ -*noun* Work, especially schoolwork, done at home.

hos·tile /hŏs´ təl/ -*adj.* Openly and strongly unfriendly: *A hostile attitude wins few friends.*

hour /our/ -*noun* An amount of time equal to sixty minutes; one twenty-fourth of a day: *Most movies are about two hours long.*

house /hous/ -*noun* A building where people live: *They need a large house because they have ten children.*

i·de·a /ī dē′ ə/ -*noun* A belief, thought, or plan in one's mind: *Jeff had an idea for saving the company money.*

im·por·tant /ĭm pôr′ tnt/ -*adj.* Having great value or worth: *Keep all your important papers in a safe place.*

in·stead /ĭn stĕd′/ -*adverb* In place of something else; rather than something else: *I took the short route instead of the long one.*

jail /jāl/ -*noun* A place where people are kept while they wait for a trial or as a punishment for a crime.

jeans /jēnz/ -*noun* Pants made from denim or another strong cloth: *Joe wears jeans to work in the garden.*

judge /jŭj/ -*noun* **1.** A person in charge of a courtroom. **2.** A person who decides the winner of a contest. -*verb* **1.** To make a decision about something. **2.** To form an opinion of something.

knee /nē/ -*noun* The part of the leg where the thigh and lower leg come together.

la·bor /lā′ bər/ -*noun* Work, especially hard work: *The labor of ironing made Chris tired.* -*verb* To work hard.

late /lāt/ -*adj.* Not on time; after expected: *If the mail is not here by lunchtime, it is late.*

laun·dry /lôn′ drē/ -*noun* Clothes that need to be or that have just been washed: *I had a large pile of laundry to do when the washer was finally fixed.*

lease /lēs/ -*noun* A written agreement between an owner and a renter: *The lease on the house is good for one year.* -*verb* To rent.

let·ter /lĕt′ ər/ -*noun* A written message: *I received a letter from my mother in this morning's mail.*

li·brar·y /lī′ brĕr′ ē/ -*noun* A place where books, films, and other materials are kept for using in the building or for borrowing: *The library lets people borrow books for two weeks.*

li·cense /lī′ səns/ -*noun* A paper showing that a person has permission to do something; a permit: *You must have a license if you want to fish in this river.*

lim·it /lĭm′ ĭt/ -*verb* To keep within a certain number or border: *The company many limit the number of sick days you can take with pay.*

lose /lōōz/ -*verb* **1.** To fail to win. **2.** To misplace, not be able to find.

loy·al /loi′ əl/ -*adj.* Strong in suppport of something; faithful: *The workers were loyal to their boss because she was always fair.*

ma·chine /mə shēn′/ -*noun* A tool with parts that work together to do a job: *Sewing with a machine is faster than sewing by hand.*

mil·i·tar·y /mĭl′ ĭ tĕr′ ē/ -*noun* The armed forces; the army, navy, and air force.

mis·take /mĭ stāk′/ -*noun* Something that is not done in the right or best way: *It would be a mistake to travel during rush hour.*

move /mōōv/ -*verb* **moved, moving, moves** **1.** To change the place where one lives: *The Smiths will move to a smaller house next spring.* **2.** To change position or place.

nec·es·sa·ry /nĕs′ ĭ sĕr′ ē/ -*adj.* Needed or required: *We have all the necessary materials to build the house.*

neigh·bor /**nā′** bər/ –*noun* Person who lives close by.

noon /nōon/ –*noun* The middle of the day; lunchtime: *The sun is hottest at noon.*

nor·mal /**nôr′** məl/ –*adj.* Usual or regular, like most others of its kind: *The normal waiting period is two weeks, but it could be more or less.*

note·book /**nōt′** bŏŏk′/ –*noun* A book with pages for writing on.

of·fice /**ô′** fĭs/ –*noun* **1.** A public job or position: *Three people are running for the office of president.* **2.** A place of business or a place where work is done.

of·ten /**ô′** fən/ –*adverb* Many times; frequently: *I often go for coffee during my break.*

ounce /ouns/ –*noun* A unit for measuring weight equal to one sixteenth of a pound.

out·line /**out′** līn′/ –*noun* A summary of the points: *Make an outline of your speech to help you remember the important points.*

o·ver·look /**ō′** vər **lŏŏk′**/ –*verb* **1.** To fail to see or notice. **2.** To look down on from a higher level.

pack·age /**păk′** ĭj/ –*noun* A box, case, or parcel with one or more things inside: *Grandma sent us a package of her best recipes.*

paint /pānt/ –*verb* To cover or coat with liquid color that dries hard: *If we paint the house red, it will look like a barn.*

par·ent /**păr′** ənt/ –*noun* A mother or father.

part·y /**pär′** tē/ –*noun* **1.** A group of people doing something together: *A party of hikers set off this morning.* **2.** A political organization. **3.** A celebration.

peace /pēs/ –*noun* **1.** Freedom from war. **2.** Freedom from worry.

peculiar /pi **kyōōl′** yər/ –*adj.* Unusual, strange, or relating to one person, place, or thing: *His peculiar hairstyle attracted attention.*

pen·ny /**pĕn′** ē/ –*noun* A coin with a value of one cent.

peo·ple /**pē′** pəl/ –*noun* Human beings; men, women, and children. *The room was full of people waiting to see the doctor.*

per·fect /**pûr′** fĭkt/ –*adj.* Without flaw or mistakes: *Jen was surprised by her perfect score; she expected to get one or two answers wrong.*

per·form /pər **fôrm′**/ –*verb* **1.** To carry out, do: *We will perform three steps to make these tools.* **2.** To do something in front of people: *Jill will perform a dance at the show.*

per·haps /pər **hăps′**/ –*adverb* Maybe: *If the rain comes, perhaps we will have a good crop this year.*

per·il /**pĕr′** əl/ –*noun* Danger or risk of harm: *The hikers were in peril in the high winds.*

po·lice /pə **lēs′**/ –*noun* People who make sure laws are obeyed.

pow·er /**pou′** ər/ –*noun* **1.** The ability, strength, or energy to do something. **2.** Influence or authority.

pride /prīd/ –*noun* **1.** A feeling of dignity or worth. **2.** Pleasure in something that one did or that one owns.

prob·lem /**prŏb′** ləm/ –*noun* Something that causes trouble or difficulty: *Now that we solved the problem with the fan belt, the machine works fine.*

prop·er /**prŏp′** ər/ –*adj.* Correct; appropriate; suitable: *Hospital workers know the proper way to make a bed.*

proud /proud/ –*adj.* Feeling happy or satisfied about something: *Justin was proud of winning the race.*

prove /pro͞ov/ –*verb* **proved, proved** *or* **proven, proving, proves** To show to be true or correct: *Can you prove that you were not in town the night of the crime?*

pur·pose /pûr′ pəs/ –*noun* A goal or aim; the desired result: *The purpose of the meeting is to answer questions about the health plan.*

quart /kwôrt/ –*noun* A unit for measuring liquids; equal to two pints.

ques·tion /kwĕs′ chən/ –*noun* Something that is asked: *After the workshop, the speaker will answer our questions.*

rea·son /rē′ zən/ –*noun* **1.** The cause for an action. **2.** An explanation. **3.** The ability to think clearly and logically.

re·call /rĭ kôl′/ *or* /rē′ kôl/ –*verb* **1.** To call back; ask for something to be returned. **2.** To bring back to mind; remember.

re·ceive /rĭ sēv′/ –*verb* **received, receiving, receives** To get or accept: *Steve always receives lots of cards on his birthday.*

re·cov·er /rĭ kŭv′ ər/ –*verb* **1.** To get back. **2.** To return to normal: *It took Dan two days to recover from his fall off the ladder.*

re·fuse /rĭ fyo͞oz′/ –*verb* **refused, refusing, refuses 1.** To be unwilling to do or give something: *I refuse to give up my seat on the bus.* **2.** To reject something that is offered.

re·mem·ber /rĭ mĕm′ bər/ –*verb* To bring back to mind; recall: *Will you remember to bring the pictures to Rob?*

rent /rĕnt/ –*verb* To use in exchange for a payment: *We will rent a car when we go to Florida.*

repeat /rĭ pēt′/ –*verb* To say or do again: *Stan will repeat the exercise until he gets it right.*

re·port /rĭ pôrt′/ –*noun* An account or description of something: *The report shows that sales are up this year.*

re·quire /rĭ kwīr′/ –*verb* **required, requiring, requires 1.** To order or demand: *This class requires a lot of reading.* **2.** To need.

res·cue /rĕs′ kyo͞o/ –*verb* **rescued, rescuing, rescues** To save from danger or harm: *The firefighters will rescue the children first and then the pets.*

re·turn /rĭ tûrn′/ –*verb* **1.** To go or come back to: *We will return home after a short vacation.* **2.** To give back.

re·view /rĭ vyo͞o′/ –*verb* To go over or look at again; to study.

re·ward /rĭ wôrd′/ –*noun* A gift or prize given for service or to mark an accomplishment: *She got a medal as a reward for her loyal service to the company.*

risk /rĭsk/ –*noun* The chance of loss or harm: *What is the risk of losing your boat in the storm?*

school /sko͞ol/ –*noun* A place for teaching and learning: *The school has students in grades seven and eight only.*

sel·dom /sĕl′ dəm/ –*adverb* Not often, infrequently, rarely: *We seldom see two full moons in one month.*

sense /sĕns/ –*noun* Good judgment: *It makes sense to carry an umbrella on a rainy day.*

shrink /shrĭngk/ –*verb* **shrank** *or* **shrunk, shrunk** *or* **shrunken, shrinking, shrinks** To make or become smaller: *Cotton clothes often shrink in the dryer.*

sim·ple /sĭm′ pəl/ –*adj.* Not hard or complex: *Sometimes a simple answer to a problem is a good one.*

skill /skĭl/ *-noun* The ability to do something well.

skin /skĭn/ *-noun* The organ that covers the body of people and animals.

speech /spēch/ *-noun* **1.** A talk given in public. **2.** The act of saying something with words.

squeeze /skwēz/ *-verb* **squeezed, squeezing, squeezes** To press together: *Squeeze the orange to make orange juice.*

stom·ach /stŭm' ək/ *-noun* The part of the body where food goes when it is swallowed and that starts breaking food down for use by the body.

straight /strāt/ *-adverb* Right away, directly: *The judge sent the robber straight to jail. -adj.* Without a bend or break.

strong /strông/ *-adj.* Having power, energy, or strength: *You must be strong to run a very long race.*

stud·y /stŭd' ē/ *-verb* **studied, studying, studies** To try to learn: *Tom plans to study for the license exam all week.*

style /stīl/ *-noun* A special way of doing or making something: *His style of writing made his books easy to read.*

sug·ar /shoog' ər/ *-noun* A sweet white or brown powder usually made from sugar beets or sugarcane.

sum·mer /sŭm' ər/ *-noun* The season of warm weather between spring and autumn.

sup·port /sə pôrt'/ *-noun* A person or thing that holds something up and keeps it from falling. *-verb* **1.** To hold something up. **2.** To help.

sure /shoor/ *-adj.* Certain, without a doubt: *Can you be sure you left your glasses here?*

sur·vive /sər vīv'/ *-verb* **survived, surviving, survives** To live through; stay alive: *Tracy was lucky to survive the flood; many people died.*

sweet /swēt/ *-adj.* Having a pleasing taste like that of sugar: *The candy was sweet and delicious.*

tal·ent /tăl' ənt/ *-noun* An ability one is born with; a natural ability: *She has a talent for singing that will get better with training.*

tem·per·a·ture /těm' pər ə chər'/ *-noun* The hotness or coldness of something as measured on a standard scale: *The temperature of the house went down quickly when the heater broke.*

their /thâr/ *-pronoun* Of or belonging to them: *Their house is the last one on the right.*

thor·ough /thûr' ō/ *-adj.* Complete, not overlooking anything; careful: *After a thorough cleaning, the bike looked like it was new.*

thought /thôt/ *-noun* **1.** The act of thinking. **2.** The result of thinking; an idea.

tick·et /tĭk' ĭt/ *-noun* **1.** A notice that a person has broken the law: *The police gave me a ticket for driving too fast.* **2.** A paper that gives someone a privilege or a service.

to·geth·er /tə gĕth' ər/ *-adverb* Along with others.

tongue /tŭng/ *-noun* A movable part of the mouth used in eating and speaking.

toward /tôrd/, /tōrd/ or /tə wôrd'/ *-preposition* In the direction of: *We looked toward the door when we heard a noise in the hall.*

traf·fic /trăf' ĭk/ *-noun* Vehicles and people moving along the street, sidewalk, water, or in the air.

trag·e·dy /trăj' ĭ dē/ *-noun* A very bad happening or event; a disaster: *The flood was a tragedy for everyone living near the river.*

train /trān/ -noun A line of railroad cars connected to each other and pulled by an engine.

trav·el /trăv′ əl/ -verb To go from one place to another: *It takes many hours to travel from New York to Hawaii.*

trou·ble /trŭb′ əl/ -noun Difficulty or danger: *Driving on the wrong side of the road can get you in trouble.*

trou·sers /trou′ zərz/ -noun A piece of clothing covering from the waist to the ankles and divided to fit around each leg separately; pants: *Ken needs a belt to keep his trousers from falling down.*

truth /trooth/ -noun Something that is correct or true: *You must always tell the truth in court.*

un·der·stand /ŭn′ dər stănd′/ -verb **understood, understanding, understands** To get the meaning of; to know: *Always let your boss know if you do not understand what you are supposed to do.*

un·famil·iar /ŭn′ fə mĭl′ yər/ -adj. Not seen or heard by many people or very often; not known by many people: *We heard an unfamiliar noise coming from the car engine.*

u·su·al /yoo′ zhoo əl/ -adj. Common or as expected: *The usual price is $5.00, but I saw it on sale for $3.00.*

vi·brate /vī′ brāt′/ -verb **vibrated, vibrating, vibrates** To move or cause to move back and forth very quickly: *The fast train made the windows vibrate.*

vic·to·ry /vĭk′ tə rē/ -noun The winning of a contest; success.

vis·it /vĭz′ ĭt/ -verb To go to see: *We try to visit the old farm once a year.*

vote /vōt/ -verb **voted, voting, votes** To make one's choice known by a ballot, voice, or show of hands.

weak /wēk/ -adj. Not having power, energy, or strength; not strong: *Carl felt weak when he had the flu.*

week /wēk/ -noun A period of seven days.

weight /wāt/ -noun The heaviness of an object or person: *The weight of a bag of sugar is ten pounds.*

when·ev·er /hwĕn ĕv′ ər/ -adverb At any time when: *We can go whenever you are ready.*

wheth·er /hwĕth′ ər/ -conjunction **1.** If: *I'm not sure whether we will get to the store on time.* **2.** Used to introduce a choice or possibilities.

win·dow /wĭn′ dō/ -noun An opening in a wall that one can see through and that lets in air and light: *Close the window before it starts to rain.*

world /wûrld/ -noun The earth: *The sailor is planning a trip around the world.*

wrin·kle /rĭng′ kəl/ -verb **wrinkled, wrinkling, wrinkles** To make small folds or lines; to crease. -noun A small fold or line.

Personal Word List

Write any words that need more study. You can write words you see in this book, at work, or at home.

Alphabetical Word List

Word	Lesson	Word	Lesson	Word	Lesson
able	21	bounce	4	daily	14
about	22	bridge	16	dairy	2
above	16	brief	5	danger	11
absent	10	brought	11	date	21
achieve	15	burn	7	deadline	10
active	9	butter	2	decide	22
afraid	24	cafeteria	9	declare	17
agree	10	camp	13	defend	18
allow	12	care	6	delay	14
almost	11	careless	11	deliver	14
alone	23	category	8	demand	21
already	4	caught	5	destroy	20
although	12	cautious	1	detail	23
always	11	cereal	8	devotion	19
among	12	chance	22	dollar	4
another	5	change	24	double	12
answer	14	children	13	doubt	13
apply	9	choice	1	early	14
arrive	9	choose	18	earn	12
assist	7	circle	16	easy	10
awful	18	city	14	either	13
back	5	clean	7	employer	9
banana	8	clinic	6	enough	3
bathe	6	clock	9	escape	20
battle	19	coin	4	event	10
beach	13	collar	3	eyes	5
because	11	confuse	22	fact	23
beginning	21	contain	8	familiar	8
belief	17	cook	9	family	1
below	21	cost	10	field	19
bicycle	6	country	16	final	17
body	6	course	15	fine	18
book	15	crime	18	finger	6
bought	1	crumb	2	finish	21

Word	Lesson	Word	Lesson	Word	Lesson
flour	2	lose	17	prove	19
foe	20	loyal	20	purpose	22
foolish	24	machine	4	quart	2
forget	21	military	20	question	15
fruit	8	mistake	16	reason	24
goggles	11	move	1	recall	22
grain	8	necessary	14	receive	2
group	21	neighbor	1	recover	7
guess	2	noon	15	refuse	24
habit	6	normal	14	remember	21
half	19	notebook	22	rent	1
handbook	12	office	17	repeat	6
handle	11	often	13	report	10
height	3	ounce	2	require	2
highway	16	outline	23	rescue	7
homework	15	overlook	24	return	23
hostile	18	package	14	review	23
hour	23	paint	9	reward	12
house	1	parent	13	risk	7
idea	22	party	17	school	9
important	16	peace	20	seldom	6
instead	8	peculiar	3	sense	22
jail	18	penny	4	shrink	3
jeans	3	people	12	simple	22
judge	18	perfect	11	skill	24
knee	5	perform	10	skin	7
labor	9	perhaps	12	speech	17
late	10	peril	7	squeeze	6
laundry	4	police	20	stomach	8
lease	1	power	24	straight	1
letter	14	pride	19	strong	20
library	13	problem	15	study	15
license	16	proper	23	style	3
limit	21	proud	13	sugar	2

Word	Lesson	Word	Lesson
summer	13	world	19
support	7	wrinkle	3
sure	23		
survive	19		
sweet	8		
talent	24		
temperature	5		
their	19		
thorough	17		
thought	24		
ticket	18		
together	20		
tongue	5		
toward	11		
traffic	18		
tragedy	7		
train	16		
travel	16		
trouble	20		
trousers	4		
truth	19		
understand	23		
unfamiliar	3		
usual	10		
vibrate	4		
victory	17		
visit	15		
vote	17		
weak	5		
week	12		
weight	3		
whenever	15		
whether	5		
window	4		

Answer Key

Pre-test

Page 10: 1. B, 2. B, 3. D, 4. C, 5. B, 6. D, 7. A, 8. C, 9. C, 10. D

Page 11: 11. B, 12. A, 13. D, 14. B, 15. A, 16. C, 17. B, 18. C, 19. B, 20. A, 21. C, 22. B, 23. A, 24. A, 25. D, 26. C, 27. D, 28. B, 29. C, 30. A

Unit 1, Lesson 1

Page 12: 1. cautious, 2. lease, 3. move, 4. bought, 5. straight, 6. rent, 7. neighbor, 8. house, 9. family, 10. choice

Page 13: 1. rent, 2. cautious, 3. choice, 4. bought, 5. lease, 6. straight, 7. e, o, neighbor; 8. o, u, house; 9. i, y, family; 10. o, e, move; 11. cautious, 12. family, 13. move, 14. choice, 15. bought, 16. neighbor, 17. rent, 18. lease

Page 14: 1. family, move, rent; 2. apple, grape, lemon; 3. bend, sit, stand; 4. lease, map, money; 5. hill, house, yard; 6. bake, break, straight; 7. car, check, clerk; 8. rail, room, rub

Page 15: house, neighbor, lease

Lesson 2

Page 16: 1. sugar, 2. quart, 3. require, 4. dairy, 5. crumb, 6. receive, 7. guess, 8. flour, 9. ounce, 10. butter

Page 17: 1. guess, butter; 2. dairy, 3. crumb, flour; 4. receive, 5. flour, 6. ounce, 7. require, receive; 8. receive, 9. sugar, 10. guess, 11. dairy, 12. quart, 13. butter, 14. guess, guess; 15. raquire, require; 16. b, crumb; 17. u, guess; 18. a, i, dairy

Page 18: 1. choice, 2. sug•ar, 3. dair•y, 4. re•quire, 5. house, 6. fam•i•ly, 7. rent, 8. re•ceive, 9. bod•y, 10. guess, 11. e•nough, 12. be•fore, 13. fish, 14. ba•con, 15. win•dow, 16. yel•low, 17. sand•wich, 18. dark, 19. mem•ber, 20. hus•band, 21. hap•pi•ness, 22. af•ter•noon

Page 19: dairy, quart, receive

Lesson 3

Page 20: 1. enough, 2. style, 3. unfamiliar, 4. jeans, 5. wrinkle, 6. collar, 7. height, 8. unfamiliar, 9. shrink, 10. weight

Page 21: 1. lar, collar; 2. liar, peculiar; 3. nough, enough; 4. mil, unfamiliar; 5. jeans, 6. weight, height; 7. wrinkle, style; 8. shrink, 9. peculiar, unfamiliar; 10. collar, 11. wrinkle, 12. collar, enough; 13. shrink, 14–18. weight, jeans, style, shrink, height

Page 22: 1. lead, 2. heal, 3. dear, 4. wait, 5. led, 6. here, 7. creak, 8. heel

Page 23: collar, wrinkle, peculiar

Lesson 4

Page 24: 1. dollar, 2. already, 3. laundry, 4. penny, 5. bounce, 6. vibrate, 7. machine, 8. coin, 9. trousers, 10. window

Page 25: 1. l, a, dollar; 2. n, penny; 3. u, r, laundry; 4. u, c, bounce; 5. c, i, machine; 6. o, i, coin; 7. already, 8. dollar, 9. already, 10. dollar, penny; 11. window, 12. vibrate, 13. trousers, 14. coin, bounce; 15–20. vi•brate, trou•sers, dol•lar, pen•ny, laun•dry, win•dow

Page 26: 1. machines, 2. toolboxes, 3. directions, 4. dishes, 5. branches, 6. shirts, 7. glasses, 8. houses

Page 27: laundry, already, dollar

Unit 1 Review

Page 28: 1. C, 2. B, 3. A, 4. B, 5. D, 6. A, 7. C, 8. C, 9. A, 10. C

Page 29: 11. C, 12. B, 13. A, 14. D, 15. D, 16. C, 17. A, 18. B, 19. D, 20. B

Unit 2, Lesson 5

Page 30: 1. caught, 2. weak, 3. brief, 4. knee, 5. whether, 6. tongue, 7. eyes, 8. another, 9. back, 10. temperature

Page 31: 1. knee, 2. another, 3. brief, 4. caught, 5. eyes, 6. whether, another; 7. temperature, 8. back,

9. tongue, 10. weak, 11–17. (brief), weak, (knee), tongue, eyes, back, caught; 18. y, s, eyes; 19. g, h, caught; 20. u, e, tongue; 21. a, u, temperature; 22. h, e, whether

Page 32: clim(b), lis(t)en; 3. ans(w)er, 4. (w)rong, 5. ca(l)f, 6. thum(b), 7. de(b)ts, 8. s(c)issors, 9. (w)rist, 10. (k)nob, 11. (k)not, 12. cas(t)le, 13. (h)onor, 14. (k)nit, 15. lim(b), 16. lam(b), 17. g(h)ost, 18. (k)nuckle, 19. si(g)n, 20. g(u)est

Page 33: temperature, caught, weak

Lesson 6

Page 34: 1. fingers, 2. clinic, 3. habit, 4. bathe, 5. care, 6. body, 7. seldom, 8. bicycle, 9. repeat, 10. squeeze

Page 35: 1. seldom, 2. body, 3. clinic, 4. habit, 5. finger, 6. bicycle, 7. repeat, 8. squeeze, 9. body, 10. bathe, 11. care, 12. repeat, 13. clinic, 14. bicycle, 15. finger, 16. bathe, 17. bicycle, 18. body, 19. care, 20. clinic

Page 36: 1. looked, 2. asking, 3. adding, 4. stayed, 5. talked, 6. washing, 7. mixed, 8. pouring, 9. guessed, 10. boiling, 11. shrinking, 12. explained, 13. We asked the crew leader for the day off yesterday. 14. She rushed to the clinic to get help an hour ago. 15. Try doing some exercises every day. 16. The nurse repeated the directions several times.

Page 37: bicycle, bathe, squeeze

Lesson 7

Page 38: 1. recover, 2. peril, 3. rescue, 4. burn, 5. skin, 6. clean, 7. assist, 8. support, 9. tragedy, 10. risk

Page 39: 1. support, assist; 2. recover, 3. clean, 4. tragedy, 5. assist, 6. burn, 7. skin, 8. burn, 9. clean, 10. risk, 11. e, i, peril; 12. e, c, rescue; 13. tragedy, 14. support, 15. peril, 16. recover

Page 40: 1. dancing, 2. grabbing, 3. rubbed, 4. pleased, 5. caring, 6. wrapped, 7. The cook was squeezing the juice form the lemons. 8. She spotted the water boiling on the stove. 9. The hot grease dropped on the stove. 10. Smoke began rising from the trash. 11. People began running for the doors. 12. The flames were whipped by the winds.

Page 41: support, tragedy, Assist, getting

Lesson 8

Page 42: 1. grain, 2. stomach, 3. instead, 4. fruit, 5. category, 6. banana, 7. familiar, 8. sweet, 9. cereal, 10. contain

Page 43: 1–3. sw(ee)t, gr(ai)n, fr(ui)t; 4–6. in•stead, con•tain, sto•mach; 7. familiar, 8. cereal, 9. category, 10. banana, 11. sweet, 12. contain, 13. fruit, 14. grain, 15. (stomack), stomach; 16. (insted), instead; 17. (familier), familiar; 18. (catagory), category

Page 44: 1. cities, 2. hobbies, 3. babies, 4. puppies, 5. cried, 6. hurried, 7. dried, 8. copied, 9. Three families came to the school. 10. We have tried to eat less fat and more fruit. 11. The worker had hurried to the bus stop. 12. Make seven copies of the page. 13. The storms were followed by blue skies. 14. The wet towels dried in the sun yesterday.

Page 45: categories, cereal, stomach, instead

Unit 2 Review

Page 46: 1. D, 2. B, 3. A, 4. C, 5. C, 6. D, 7. A, 8. C, 9. B, 10. A, 11. C, 12. B

Page 47: 13. B, 14. C, 15. D, 16. A, 17. C, 18. D, 19. B, 20. A, 21. D, 22. B, 23. C, 24. A

Unit 3, Lesson 9

Page 48: 1. apply, 2. arrive, 3. school, 4. cook, 5. employer, 6. clock, 7. active, 8. cafeteria, 9. labor, 10. paint

Page 49: 1. apply, arrive; 2. cook, school; 3. employer, 4. active, 5. clock, 6. cafeteria, 7. labor, 8. clock, paint; 9–12. ap•ply, ar•rive, ac•tive, la•bor; 13. te, cafeteria; 14. ploy, employer; 15. ac, active; 16. ar, arrive; 17. bor, labor; 18. ply, apply

Page 50: 1. helper, 2. camper, 3. singer, 4. writer, 5. fighter, 6. skater, 7. healer, 8. teacher, 9. pitcher,

10. speaker, **11.** farmer, **12.** cheerleader
Page 51: cafeteria, labor, arrive

Lesson 10

Page 52: **1.** deadline, **2.** cost, **3.** absent, **4.** usual,
5. perform, **6.** event, **7.** report, **8.** easy, **9.** agree, **10.** late
Page 53: **1.** e, absent; **2.** u, a, usual; **3.** e, o, perform;
4. s, easy; **5.** a, i, deadline; **6.** e, e, event; **7.** deadline,
8. cost, **9.** absent, **10.** late, **11.** event, **12.** report,
13. agree, **14.** report, **15.** event, **16.** usual, **17.** perform,
18. cost
Page 54: **1.** redo, **2.** unwanted, **3.** unfair, **4.** rewrap,
5. repaint, **6.** uneven, **7.** rebuild, **8.** unhappy, **9.** repack,
10. unpack, **11.** reorder, **12.** unwind, **13.** reorder, Our
order was lost. I will have to reorder the book.
14. unpaid, Joe was not paid for the work. He is an
unpaid worker. **15.** refill, Marie spilled the milk.
She had to refill her glass.
Page 55: perform, easy, usual

Lesson 11

Page 56: **1.** because, **2.** brought, **3.** almost, **4.** goggles,
5. handle, **6.** danger, **7.** toward, **8.** always, **9.** perfect,
10. careless
Page 57: **1.** toward, **2.** danger, **3.** almost, **4.** goggles,
5. careless, **6.** perfect, **7.** brought, **8.** always,
9. goggles, **10.** handle, **11.** toward, **12.** because,
13. careless, **14.** always, almost; **15.** handle, **16.** danger
Page 58: **1.** useless, **2.** useful, **3.** hopeless, **4.** hopeful,
5. thankful, **6.** doubtless, **7.** truthful, **8.** endless,
9. flavorless, **10.** fearful, **11.** The prancing horses
were graceful. **12.** The matches were useless after
they got wet.
Page 59: goggles, careless, almost

Lesson 12

Page 60: **1.** week, **2.** double, **3.** earn, **4.** handbook,
5. although, **6.** reward, **7.** allow, **8.** perhaps, **9.** among,
10. people
Page 61: **1.** allow, **2.** although, **3.** handbook, **4.** people,

double; **5.** week, handbook; **6.** earn, week; **7.** allow,
although; **8.** double, **9.** e, a, reward; **10.** a, o, among;
11. h, a, perhaps; **12.** e, a, earn; **13.** u, l, double;
14. o, l, people, **15.** (prehaps), perhaps;
16. (amung), among; **17.** (hanbook), handbook;
18. (rewerd), reward
Page 62: **1.** maybe, **2.** nobody, **3.** without, **4.** football,
5. birthday, **6.** grandmother, **7.** homesick, **8.** forever,
9. bedroom, **10.** railroad, **11.** daylight, **12.** everything,
13. outside, Put on your coat before going outside.
14. homesick, After a week at camp, she became
homesick. **15.** forever, We waited for thirty
minutes, but it seemed like forever.
Page 63: week, Perhaps, double

Unit 3 Review

Page 64: **1.** B, **2.** C, **3.** A, **4.** C, **5.** A, **6.** B, **7.** A, **8.** D,
9. B, **10.** B, **11.** C, **12.** D
Page 65: **13.** B, **14.** D, **15.** D, **16.** A, **17.** C, **18.** B, **19.** C,
20. D, **21.** C, **22.** C, **23.** A, **24.** D

Lesson 13

Page 66: **1.** parent, **2.** doubt, **3.** library, **4.** often,
5. camp, **6.** children, **7.** either, **8.** proud, **9.** summer,
10. beach
Page 67: **1.** r, r, library; **2.** t, e, often; **3.** i, e, either;
4. m, e, summer; **5.** l, e, children; **6.** a, e, parent;
7. o, u, proud; **8.** doubt, proud, camp, beach;
9. beach, **10.** doubt, **11.** either, summer; **12.** often,
children; **13.** library, **14.** doubt, proud; **15.** summer,
16. camp, **17–18.** children, proud
Page 68: **1.** men, The man called a meeting. Many
men were there. **2.** mouse, The mice were in a
cage. One mouse was white. **3.** tooth, Except for
one tooth, all her teeth were fine. **4.** foot, Everyone's
feet hurt. My left foot was very sore. **5.** children,
One child is missing. There should be five
children here. **6.** woman, We studied many great
women. One woman, Mother Teresa, stood out.
7. geese, One goose escaped. We still had four
geese left. **8.** oxen, An ox took a day to do the

work. Four oxen did it in an hour.
Page 69: SUMMER, either, library

Lesson 14

Page 70: 1. letter, **2.** daily, **3.** normal, **4.** delay,
5. answer, **6.** necessary, **7.** city, **8.** package, **9.** early,
10. deliver
Page 71: 1. y, city; **2.** let, letter; **3.** an, answer; **4.** de,
delay; **5.** letter, necessary; **6.** deliver, **7.** early, daily;
8. city, **9.** necessary, **10.** answer, **11–13.** daily, delay,
deliver; **14.** (necesary), necessary; **15.** (packege),
package; **16.** (normel), normal
Page 72: 1. Manuel Perez, **2.** 2845 West Allen
Road, **3.** Phoenix, **4.** 85006, **5.** Eduardo Santos,
6. 744 Second Avenue, **7.** Pima, **8.** 85535, **9.** yes,
10. stamp
Page 73: package, delivered, early

Lesson 15

Page: 74: 1. homework, **2.** course, **3.** achieve,
4. problem, **5.** book, **6.** study, **7.** visit, **8.** whenever,
9. noon, **10.** question
Page 75: 1. book, noon; **2.** homework, whenever;
3. question, noon; **4.** achieve, **5.** study, **6.** l, e,
problem; **7.** o, s, course; **8.** i, i, visit; **9.** e, t, question;
10. u, y, study; **11.** book, **12.** achieve, **13.** course,
14. visit
Page 76: 1. e, i, eight; **2.** i, e, thief; **3.** i, e, review;
4. i, e, die; **5.** i, e, chief; **6.** e, i, neither; **7.** e, i,
ceiling; **8.** i, e, science; **9.** i, e, niece; **10.** i, e, belief;
11. i, e, pie; **12.** i, e, yield; **13.** i, e, achieve; **14.** i, e,
tie, **15.** e, i, receive; **16.** e, i, seize
Page 77: visit, homework, achieve

Lesson 16

Page 78: 1. country, **2.** travel, **3.** mistake, **4.** highway,
5. bridge, **6.** train, **7.** above, **8.** important, **9.** license,
10. circle
Page 79: 1. bridge, **2.** mistake, **3.** train, **4.** above,
5. highway, **6.** license, **7.** travel, **8.** circle,

9. important, **10.** country, **11–13.** train, bridge,
(travel); **14.** c, s, license; **15.** o, a, important; **16.** i, l,
circle; **17.** o, r, country; **18.** a, o, above
Page 80: 1. This, **2.** Never. . . I, **3.** We, **4.** Now I,
5. She, **6.** Will I, **7.** You, **8.** If I, **9.** This, **10.** Tammy
. . . I
Page 81: bridge, Large, circle, important

Unit 4 Review

Page 82: 1. C, **2.** A, **3.** C, **4.** A, **5.** B, **6.** C, **7.** A, **8.** D,
9. B, **10.** D, **11.** A, **12.** B
Page 83: 13. C, **14.** B, **15.** A, **16.** D, **17.** B, **18.** C, **19.** A,
20. B, **21.** C, **22.** D, **23.** A, **24.** B

Unit 5, Lesson 17

Page 84: 1. party, **2.** vote, **3.** final, **4.** belief, **5.** lose,
6. speech, **7.** victory, **8.** declare, **9.** final, **10.** office
Page 85: 1. thorough, **2.** office, **3.** victory, **4.** speech,
thorough; **5.** party, **6.** belief, **7.** vote, **8.** declare,
9. declare, office, vote, lose; **10.** nal, final; **11.** to,
victory; **12.** par, party; **13.** (luse), lose; **14.** (speach),
speech; **15.** (fynal), final; **16.** (declair), declare
Page 86: 1. Four people are running for that office.
2. Do you belong to a political party? **3.** What a
great speech! **4.** It is your duty to vote. **5.** Has he
been declared the winner? **6.** Did you do a
thorough study of the problem? **7.** A victory party
is planned for tonight. **8.** Look out!
Page 87: party, Do . . . change?, belief, final

Lesson 18

Page 88: 1. choose **2.** ticket, **3.** crime, **4.** fine, **5.** judge,
6. defend, **7.** hostile, **8.** jail, **9.** traffic, **10.** awful
Page 89: 1. o, o, choose; **2.** f, f, traffic; **3.** a, w, awful;
4. e, e, defend; **5.** d, g, judge; **6.** i, l, hostile; **7.** i, e,
crime; **8.** c, e, ticket; **9.** judge, **10.** traffic, **11.** awful,
12. ticket, **13.** defend, **14.** jail, **15.** defend,
16–20. (choose), jail, (fine), (crime), judge
Page 90: 1. Judge Wang, **2.** Uncle Tom, **3.** Ms. Amy
Rodman, **4.** no capitals, **5.** Dr. Wagner, **6.** no

capitals, **7.** Mr. Simmons, **8.** Captain Dawson,
9. no capitals, **10.** Ms. Ripkin's
Page 91: Judge, ticket, defend, choose

Lesson 19

Page 92: 1. pride, **2.** world, **3.** field, **4.** battle, **5.** truth,
6. their, **7.** survive, **8.** devotion, **9.** half, **10.** prove
Page 93: 1. half, **2.** pride, **3.** devotion, **4.** battle,
5. field, **6.** devotion, **7.** world, field; **8.** their,
9–11. battle, devotion, survive; **12–15.** (prove),
(pride), their, truth; **16.** survive, **17.** world, **18.** truth
Page 94: 1. too, **2.** their, **3.** two, **4.** there, **5.** to,
6. two, **7.** their, **8.** too, **9.** they're, **10.** There, **11.** to,
12. They're. **13.** two, **14.** their
Page 95: their, World, field

Lesson 20

Page 96: 1. peace, **2.** together, **3.** foe, **4.** military,
5. strong, **6.** loyal, **7.** trouble, **8.** police, **9.** destroy,
10. escape
Page 97: 1. strong, **2.** foe, **3.** loyal, **4.** police, **5.** peace,
6. escape, **7.** strong, **8.** trouble, **9.** loyal, destroy;
10. escape, loyal; **11.** strong, foe, peace; **12.** destroy,
13–14. to•geth•er, mil•i•tar•y; **15.** o, l, trouble; **16.** i, a,
military; **17.** o, i, police; **18.** e, e, together
Page 98: 1. Ulysses S. Grant, **2.** Paris, France;
3. Mount Rushmore, **4.** Declaration of
Independence, **5.** Labor Day, **6.** Dallas Police
Department, **7.** Hamilton Garden Club, **8.** Davis
Street Bridge
Page 99: military, peace, Korean, escape

Unit 5 Review

Page 100: 1. D, **2.** B, **3.** C, **4.** A, **5.** B, **6.** D, **7.** B, **8.** A,
9. C, **10.** D, **11.** A, **12.** D
Page 101: 13. B, **14.** D, **15.** C, **16.** A, **17.** D, **18.** A,
19. C, **20.** B, **21.** B, **22.** A. **23.** C, **24.** D

Unit 6, Lesson 21

Page 102: 1. below, **2.** beginning, **3.** demand, **4.** able,
5. date, **6.** group, **7.** remember, **8.** limit, **9.** finish,
10. forget
Page 103: 1–5. able, demand, finish, limit, below;
6. remember, beginning; **7.** date, **8.** group, **9.** demand,
finish, beginning; **10.** beginning, **11.** remember,
12. forget, **13.** date, **14.** below, **15.** able, **16.** group,
17. finish, **18.** forget, **19.** limit, **20.** demand
Page 104: Heading will vary. Inside Address, Ms.
Joan Kirkwood, The Book Trader, 454 West
Avenue, Belleville, IL 60023. Greeting: Dear Ms.
Kirkwood. Closing and Signature will vary.
Page 105: remember, finish, forget

Lesson 22

Page 106: 1. recall, **2.** sense, **3.** about, **4.** simple,
5. confuse, **6.** chance, **7.** notebook, **8.** idea, **9.** purpose,
10. decide
Page 107: 1. sense, **2.** recall, **3.** simple, **4.** about,
5. confuse, **6.** decide, **7.** notebook, **8.** chance, **9.** recall,
10. purpose, sense; **11.** idea, **12.** chance, **13.** notebook,
14. recall, **15.** sense, **16.** about, **17.** de•cide, **18.** pur•pose,
19. re•call, **20.** sim•ple
Page 108: 1. sim-ple, **2.** de-cide, **3.** par-ent,
4. sel-dom, **5.** ma-chine, **6.** stom-ach, **7.** be-cause,
8. note-book, **9.** Twenty-six people will be at the
meet-ing. They will want answers to their
questions. **10.** I need help with my home-work.
I do not know how to do number thirty-one.
11. Jerry never travels by plane. There must be a
rea-son why he dislikes planes.
Page 109: about, sense, recall

Lesson 23

Page 110: 1. proper, **2.** detail, **3.** outline, **4.** sure,
5. hour, **6.** return, **7.** understand, **8.** fact, **9.** alone,
10. review
Page 111: 1. return, **2.** understand, outline; **3.** review,

return; **4.** hour, **5.** understand, **6.** sure, **7.** alone, **8.** detail, **9.** fact, **10.** proper, **11.** de, detail; **12.** lone, alone; **13.** re, return; **14.** out, outline; **15.** er, proper; **16.** (shure), sure; **17.** (reveiw), review; **18.** (howr), hour

Page 112: 1. carefully, Please be careful on the job. Read the safety rules carefully. **2.** quietly, You must be quiet. Walk through the room quietly. **3.** sadly, Everyone seemed sad. They spoke sadly of the loss. **4.** hungrily, The dog was hungry. It hungrily gulped down the food. **5.** slowly, It was a slow ride into town. The cars slowly crawled down the highway. **6.** lazily, What a lazy cat! It lazily sleeps in the sun all day. **7.** angrily, The player became angry. He angrily slammed his bat to the ground. **8.** quickly, We need a quick meal. What can be made quickly?

Page 113: hour, alone, outline

Lesson 24

Page 114: 1. afraid, **2.** skill, **3.** refuse, **4.** foolish, **5.** overlook, **6.** talent, **7.** power, **8.** change, **9.** thought, **10.** reason

Page 115: 1. skill, **2.** overlook, **3.** thought, **4.** foolish, **5.** thought, **6.** skill, **7.** change, **8.** afraid, **9.** pow•er, **10.** rea•son, **11.** re•fuse, **12.** tal•ent, **13.** w, e, power; **14.** e, s, refuse; **15.** e, n, talent; **16.** a, o, reason; **17.** e, o, overlook; **18.** a, e, change; **19.** f, o, h, foolish; **20.** r, d, afraid

Page 116: 1. skill, **2.** sure, **3.** fact, **4.** quick, **5.** strong, **6.** ready, **7.** forget, **8.** above, **9.** earn, **10.** brought, **11.** cheer, **12.** almost, **13.** mistake, **14.** judge, **15.** awful

Page 117: afraid, refuse, reason

Unit 6 Review

Page 118: 1. B, **2.** A, **3.** D, **4.** B, **5.** A, **6.** D, **7.** B, **8.** A, **9.** C, **10.** B, **11.** D, **12.** A

Page 119: 13. C, **14.** D, **15.** A, **16.** C. **17.** B, **18.** D, **19.** A, **20.** D, **21.** C, **22.** A, **23.** D, **24.** C

Post-test

Page 120: 1. B, **2.** D, **3.** A, **4.** C, **5.** B. **6.** A, **7.** C, **8.** A, **9.** D, **10.** B

Page 121: 11. C, **12.** B, **13.** A, **14.** B, **15.** D, **16.** C, **17.** A, **18.** B, **19.** B, **20.** A, **21.** B, **22.** D, **23.** A, **24.** C, **25.** D, **26.** D, **27.** A, **28.** B, **29.** C, **30.** D

Scoring Chart

Use this chart to find your score. Line up the number of items with the number correct.

For example, if 14 out of 15 items are correct, the score is 93.3 percent.

Number Correct

Number of Items	5	6	7	8	9	10	11	12	13	14	15	16	17	18	19	20	21	22	23	24	25	26	27	28	29	30
5	100																									
6	83.3	100																								
7	71.4	85.7	100																							
8	62.5	75	87.5	100																						
9	55.5	66.7	77.7	88.9	100																					
10	50	60	70	80	90	100																				
11	45.4	54.5	63.6	72.7	81.8	90.9	100																			
12	41.7	50	58.3	66.7	75	83.3	91.7	100																		
13	38.5	46.1	53.8	61.5	69.2	76.9	84.6	92.3	100																	
14	35.7	42.8	50	57.1	64.3	71.4	78.5	85.7	92.8	100																
15	33.3	40	46.6	53.3	60	66.7	73.3	80	86.7	93.3	100															
16	31.2	37.5	43.7	50	56.2	62.5	68.7	75	81.2	87.5	93.7	100														
17	29.4	35.3	41.2	47	52.9	58.8	64.7	70.6	76.5	82.3	88.2	94.1	100													
18	27.8	33.3	38.9	44.4	50	55.5	61.1	66.7	72.2	77.8	83.3	88.9	94.4	100												
19	26.3	31.6	36.8	42.1	47.4	52.6	57.9	63.1	68.4	73.7	78.9	84.2	89.4	94.7	100											
20	25	30	35	40	45	50	55	60	65	70	75	80	85	90	95	100										
21	23.8	28.6	33.3	38.1	42.8	47.6	52.3	57.1	61.9	66.7	71.4	76.1	80.9	85.7	90.5	95.2	100									
22	22.7	27.3	31.8	36.4	40.9	45.4	50	54.5	59.1	63.6	68.1	72.7	77.2	81.8	86.4	90.9	95.4	100								
23	21.7	26.1	30.4	34.8	39.1	43.5	47.8	52.1	56.5	60.8	65.2	69.5	73.9	78.3	82.6	86.9	91.3	95.6	100							
24	20.8	25	29.2	33.3	37.5	41.7	45.8	50	54.2	58.3	62.5	66.7	70.8	75	79.1	83.3	87.5	91.6	95.8	100						
25	20	24	28	32	36	40	44	48	52	56	60	64	68	72	76	80	84	88	92	96	100					
26	19.2	23.1	26.9	30.8	34.6	38.5	42.3	46.2	50	53.8	57.7	61.5	65.4	69.2	73.1	76.9	80.8	84.6	88.5	92.3	96.2	100				
27	18.5	22.2	25.9	29.6	33.3	37	40.7	44.4	48.1	51.9	55.6	59.2	63	66.7	70.4	74.1	77.8	81.5	85.2	88.9	92.6	96.3	100			
28	17.9	21.4	25	28.6	32.1	35.7	39.3	42.9	46.4	50	53.6	57.1	60.7	64.3	67.9	71.4	75	78.6	82.1	85.7	89.3	92.9	96.4	100		
29	17.2	20.7	24.1	27.6	31	34.5	37.9	41.4	44.8	48.3	51.7	55.2	58.6	62.1	65.5	69	72.4	75.9	79.3	82.8	86.2	89.7	93.1	96.6	100	
30	16.7	20	23.3	26.7	30	33.3	36.7	40	43.3	46.7	50	53.3	56.7	60	63.3	66.7	70	73.3	76.7	80	83.3	86.7	90	93.3	96.7	100